SO-AGT-163

Everything about this book, including the way in which it was written, is a significant departure from the way things have always been done.

Oh, and that uncomfortable feeling you get after reading it? Don't worry: That's just the sensation of having your untested assumptions dashed to smithereens. It's totally normal.

Benjamin Martin, CAE
Member Relations Director, Virginia Society of CPAs
ASAE & The Center Future Leaders Graduate
and Certified Association Executive blogger

WE HAVE ALWAYS DONE IT THAT WAY

The Five Independent Thinkers

Jeff De Cagna

C. David Gammel

Jamie Notter

Mickie Rops

Amy Smith

WE HAVE ALWAYS DONE IT THAT WAY
101 Things About Associations We Must Change

by Five Independent Thinkers

PUBLISHED BY LULU ENTERPRISES, INC.
Morrisville, North Carolina

© 2006 by Jeff De Cagna, C. David Gammel,
Jamie Notter, Mickie Rops and Amy Smith.

Some rights reserved.

This work is licensed under the Creative Commons Attribution-
NonCommercial-NoDerivs 2.5 License. To view a copy of this
license, visit http://creativecommons.org/licenses/by-nc-nd/2.5/ or
send a letter to Creative Commons, 543 Howard Street,
5th Floor, San Francisco, California, 94105, USA.

Printed in the United States of America

ISBN 978-1-84728-857-8

Prior to publication, the first draft of the content of this book
was published on a blog at http://www.alwaysdoneitthatway.com,
and after publication we will continue the conversation online.

*The Five Independent Thinkers dedicate this book
to the association community and the
tens of thousands of outstanding professionals
who try hard every day to make it better.*

We hope our work honors their efforts.

The significant problems we face
cannot be solved at the same level of thinking
we were at when we created them.

Albert Einstein

Contents

CHANGING THE WAY WE MANAGE

CHANGING THE WAY WE EXECUTE

CHANGING THE WAY WE WORK TOGETHER

CHANGING THE WAY WE INVOLVE OTHERS

Foreword

Five of the association community's brightest leaders have made it a practice to question conventional wisdom, which I believe is an essential and very healthy thing to do. I am pleased to write this foreword for *We Have Always Done It That Way: 101 Things About Associations We Must Change* for exactly that reason.

Relying on conventional wisdom is an easy way to dismiss the need for change. Oftentimes we become creatures of habit, having the same conversations year after year without taking the time to consider whether old models and approaches are still appropriate in today's world of rapid change and great uncertainty.

The exciting thought for me is that associations have so much potential to change the world for the better! We must maximize every opportunity to do just that. The question is how. We can do it by challenging ourselves to have new, different and better conversations. We can do it by questioning what we believe in, how we operate and what roles our organizations play in society. We can do it by closely examining the conventional wisdom of our profession in an honest and transparent dialogue, so we can better understand what still makes sense in today's climate and what doesn't.

The same old ways of doing business are already beginning to fail us and if we don't work toward what's next, we put our future in jeopardy. The future is full of great opportunities for associations to do what they do well, but only if energetic and capable leaders will step forward to seize the moment.

The Five Independent Thinkers writing this book—Jeff De Cagna, David Gammel, Jamie Notter, Mickie Rops and Amy Smith—are pointing our community toward ways we can break old habits and make innovation a genuine priority. I don't endorse all of the ideas and suggestions made in this book, and you probably won't agree with everything the authors recommend either. That's good. The group's goal is not to generate consensus around their solutions, but to spark controversy, create new discourse and, hopefully, identify break-through solutions. If we keep an open mind to the process of questioning conventional wisdom, I am confident we will move our professional lives and our associations to new heights. Enjoy the challenge!

Susan Sarfati, CAE
President and CEO, The Center for Association Leadership
and Executive Vice President, ASAE
July 2006

Preface

This book is different. But then you already knew that, didn't you?

Sure, we're trying to challenge the association community's status quo with these ideas. But the way we developed, wrote and published *We Have Always Done It That Way: 101 Things About Associations We Must Change* is equally a departure from the traditional rules of association publishing.

For example, although each of us is quite proud of the finished product, we chose to list "The Five Independent Thinkers" as the book's "author," rather than list our individual names on the cover. This book is about so much more than just the five of us. Yes, it was our combined initiative and hard work that created it. But we are only five of many independent thinkers who have contributed to the emerging ideas expressed in its pages, including many who influenced us without even knowing it. So it is the thinking we want to highlight here, rather than the thinkers.

The book is also unique because, as far as we know, it is the first book in the association community to begin as a weblog. Beginning in the fall of 2005, each of The Five Independent Thinkers began writing blog posts at http://www.alwaysdoneitthatway.com, items that eventually became the "101 Things About Associations We Must Change." We received reader comments over these many months and incorporated their feedback into the finished product. (Many, many thanks to everyone who commented or provided informal feedback on the blog content. We're very grateful to all of you.) Earlier this year, at ASAE & The Center's Great Ideas Conference in San Diego, we issued a prototype book with about one-third of the blog posts so we could get more input. At one point, a *We Have Always Done It That Way* blog reader and fellow blogger actually started a post for us, and we turned it into one of the 101 things in this book.

The interaction does not stop with the actual printing of the book. The blog will remain active, and we invite all book readers to check out our new posts and provide thoughtful reactions to what we have written. We hope many of yours will be among them!

The five of us would like to express our deep appreciation to everyone who has contributed to this project. At the top of this list are our collective better halves: Meeghan De Cagna, Jennifer Gammel, Liz Notter, Chris Rops and Erick Smith. Where would we be without you? We are also grateful for the editing support from Gaye Newton of Galibren Written Treasures, LLC and the graphic design support from Jennifer Gammel. Thanks also go out to Susan Sarfati for her wonderful foreword, and Kristi Graves Donovan, Nancy Green, Kevin Holland, Ben Martin and Ann Oliveri for their truly humbling testimonials.

Most of all, we want to thank you for devoting some of your time, energy and attention to the ideas presented here. We hope our book makes you think, and then inspires you to make a difference in your career, your organization and in the association community we all serve.

The Five Independent Thinkers
July 2006

Introduction: We Have Always Done It That Way

The five of us share a deep commitment to the success and growth of the association community. After all, we would not have met if each of us weren't actively involved in the work of ASAE & The Center for Association Leadership. While either working for or consulting to associations, the five of us started noticing each other while attending ASAE & The Center events, speaking at conferences or writing for association publications. From the very beginning, we recognized a common thread running through our ideas, even though we come from different disciplines and focus our work on different areas of association leadership and management.

This common thread is our view that the association community must change itself profoundly in order to succeed in a brand new world. We agree with Albert Einstein's belief that today's problems require a new level of thinking. Regardless of the focus of our work in associations, we find ourselves, in one form or another, supporting, designing, facilitating or advocating for that new thinking.

Given our worldview, when we look out at the association community today, we are disquieted by what we see. We are concerned by the instinctively conservative approach to organizational stewardship that far too many association executives and volunteers continue to pursue in the early years of the 21st century. When presented with the opportunity to take advantage of fresh ideas that can deliver new value to members and help their associations realize their full potential, too many association leaders still reflexively offer the most dreaded defense of all:

But we have always done it that way.

If we were granted the magical power to change one thing about the association community for all time, it would be to banish that phrase from our lexicon. These words, and the mindset of complacency, risk aversion and intransigence they reflect, sap the energy from our community and create nothing but frustration among those association professionals, volunteers and members who hunger for a true rebirth of our organizations. **Of the 101 things we advocate should be changed in the association community, using the "we've always done it that way" defense of the status quo tops our list.**

Beneath that overarching resistance, of course, there are hundreds and hundreds of specific association beliefs, practices and approaches that often reflect a counterproductive attachment to tradition. These ways of thinking and working also are in desperate need of change. The five of us included one hundred of the issues we think are most important in this book. We have no illusion that the list is comprehensive, nor does everything we write about involve a break with the past. Some of what we include in these pages is designed to help you better understand the future that is already emerging for our members, our organizations and the society in which live. We don't expect everyone to agree with everything we've written. In fact, we hope *you don't agree* with many of our views, and will take the time to tell us and others how you see things differently. We want to light a fire under you, in the hope that you will be moved to assist in initiating a new discourse in our community about where we go from here. It is imperative that all of us begin thinking and talking about new ways of doing things, lest our community begin to suffer the inevitable consequences of indifference. We have written this book to challenge, to provoke and to inspire. We do not claim to have all the answers (although we do propose some), but we certainly hope that we are asking the right questions.

This book is organized into six broad areas that require change: **the ways we think, lead, manage, execute, work together and involve oth-**

ers in the association community. Each author tackles issues in these categories from different angles, and each of the one hundred entries opens a new door for change, by identifying a current shortcoming or pointing to a new opportunity for moving your association forward.

As a leader, you accept at least some responsibility for what happens in your association. We encourage you to capitalize on the ideas and insights we share and use this book as a springboard to future success. We wrote this book for you and for the community we serve. If we've done our job well, over time you and association leaders across the country and around the world may choose to adopt a new default position when confronted with new ideas: **We've never done it that way, so let's try it!**

CHANGING THE WAY WE THINK

When Will We Learn?

JEFF DE CAGNA

I love questions. Far from being signs of our ignorance, questions are the pathways we take toward new understanding. So to facilitate our learning, I'd like to offer some challenging questions for thinking and conversation by leaders in our community. I grant that these questions are pointed and unmistakably reflect my perspectives on certain hot-button issues. I urge you to forget about that and simply focus on the content of each question, even if it makes you more than a little uncomfortable.

When will we learn that:

- Human beings *have always lived* in times of change?
- Today's genuine paradigm shift is deeper, faster and more intense than anything our society has experienced for more than 100 years?
- Strategic planning is NEVER, NEVER, NEVER going to help us take our organizations to the next level of success?
- Strategic planning is now a profound waste of time and resources that must be jettisoned in favor of new and different approaches that fit with a new and still shifting reality?
- The future cannot and should not be predicted?
- Our long-term success depends on cultivating a deep capacity for creating the future?
- Pursuing innovation costs less than trying to build a strong and sustainable brand?
- Being an innovator *is* a strong and sustainable brand?
- The only way to gain greater influence is to give up virtually all control?

- We never really had control in the first place?
- Demographic shift and generational shift are connected but not the same thing?
- Appreciating the meaning of generational shift requires us to admit that the life experiences of others are just as valuable as our own and worth our understanding?
- Our old assumptions about associations are already getting our organizations into trouble?
- *We* must work hard at *getting ourselves* into trouble by probing and testing these old assumptions?
- What appear to be mere technology tools today are actually the fundamental forces shaping the future of our society?
- We cannot put off embracing the transformative power of Web 2.0/social media technologies no matter how much they may subvert what we do?
- Risk cannot and should not be avoided?
- It is not possible to really lead without taking risks?
- Training and learning are not the same thing?
- We need to learn how to learn, and help our members do the same?
- "We've always done it that way" is no longer a sufficient response?
- "We've always done it that way" was never a sufficient response in the first place?

Want to make a difference in the association community? Think about these questions. Talk about them with your colleagues. Better yet, come up with your own questions. Drive the conversation everywhere you go. Make people pay attention. Don't give up and don't make excuses. Lead by choice. Lead by example. Lead with confidence.

Letting Uniqueness Stifle Growth

MICKIE ROPS

If I had a dollar for every time I've heard an association executive say their field or association is unique, this Gen Xer would be retiring soon. Not that there aren't unique elements about all our organizations, but often associations feel they are sooooo unique that they won't even consider examining other organizational strategies and models and trying to learn from them.

Associations are different than corporations; does that mean we should not even try to apply corporate experiences to our industry? Forget *The Tipping Point.* Forget *The Medici Effect.* Forget *The Long Tail.* Forget *Crucial Conversations.* Forget *The World is Flat.* The authors didn't directly study associations, so the concepts surely can't apply to us, right? **Not right.**

Bask in your uniqueness, but don't let it stifle your willingness to learn from others.

The Absence of Middle-Level Thinking

JAMIE NOTTER

Associations seem to be very good at high-level thinking. They love their vision statements and mission statements. They work hard on their keynote speeches. They really love platitudes:

- We're here for the members.
- Our priority is customer service.
- We support the development or perpetuation of the field.

Associations are equally good at details. They love their action plans. They relish the debate about the color of next year's annual meeting brochure. With a tradition of small staffs, it is not uncommon for senior managers to be immersed in the details of implementation throughout the year.

What associations really need to develop, however, is their middle-level thinking. They need to devote more time to discussing issues and making decisions that rise above the minutia of implementation, but have more subtlety or definition than the blanket statements of the mission and vision realm. Consider the following examples.

Strategy

Strategic plans typically start with the broad mission or vision and then present categories of activities, spelled out in detail. Plans basically back in to the middle level, by presenting it as the sum of all the detailed actions. Associations need to make more strategic decisions about the middle level. What really is our priority this year? Of all the things we usually do, which ones will drive our success over the next eighteen months? Those are tough decisions, but if you get clarity on them, it empowers staff to actually be more strategic during the year (rather than simply checking off to-do items from the plan).

Staff Issues

If problems or conflicts develop among staff members, the discussion tends to bounce between the high level (she's not a team player; he's not a good fit with our culture; we need her to be more of a leader) and the details (I saw her shopping online during work; he shouldn't talk to me like that during staff meeting; I can't believe she said that at a Board meeting). The opportunities for resolution, however, are in that middle level. Yes, you need to talk about the behavior, but you need to spell out how the behavior connects to those high-level conclusions. How is "team player" defined? Why, quite frankly, does everyone need to be one? What really is the culture here, and will that drive our success? What is the impact of leadership style on what we are doing? When you work through those discussions, the examination of behavior is more meaningful and effective.

Program Evaluation

There was an article in *Forum* magazine in May 2006 examining how to decide to cut long-standing programs that perfectly demonstrated the lack of a middle level. The questions they posed tended to be high level (Does this program impact the mission?) or detailed (What is the net revenue?). Those are both important, but you need some middle level analysis for this decision as well. How does this program impact our brand? Does this program help us develop internal capacity that helps us in other areas? Is this program taking resources away from our mid-level strategic direction? Without the middle level in this discussion, your evaluation tool becomes too blunt an instrument.

Embrace Heterodoxy

JEFF DE CAGNA

By circumstance, tradition or choice, associations often operate as masters of orthodoxy—the *de jure* or *de facto* enforcers of accepted ways of thinking and acting within the industries, professions and fields they serve. Through certification programs, licensing, standards and other mechanisms, associations can create near impenetrable boundaries around what professionals in those fields must, should or can know. In some respects, this is an appropriate and vital function, especially in fields in which lives are at stake.

Yet when associations place a higher priority on preserving and protecting what is known above exploring and understanding what is unknown, they may thwart the emergence of significant breakthroughs in learning and the creation of new knowledge. Associations operating as masters of orthodoxy may exclude, with or without sinister intent, divergent viewpoints that directly question accepted beliefs and conventional wisdom. But in a time of genuine paradigm shift, the tools for creating and sharing new ideas and knowledge are in the hands of many—including quite capable creators who are purely amateurs in their fields. Associations have no choice but to break down the boundaries they've created over many decades and open themselves to ideas that they might otherwise categorically reject, as well as the "dissidents" who propose them.

Heterodoxy is defined as "any opinions or doctrines at variance with the official or orthodox position." In the 21st century, associations will need to create new intellectual frameworks and environments that actively and consistently engage the broad spectrum of agreed-upon and profoundly controversial views in their fields. **Embracing heterodoxy must become the new association tradition.**

Change

Amy Smith

This posting deserves the one word title, "Change."

In the frame of "always done it that way," I would define change this way:

A painfully slow, political, arduous, tiring, grueling, time-consuming, onerous process that must involve every possible stakeholder imaginable before creating a plan to implement the change.

Why do I mock the nature of change within our community? Because all too often we ask too many people to provide input into the changes that need to be made.

Here are just a few examples.

An association is getting ready to shift the Board of Directors from a tactical board to a strategic one. The Board determines that membership feedback is important in this shift so it casts a painfully wide net and gets a predictable response. Those who sit in strong support or strong opposition state their cases loudly, but the vast majority of them do not understand the inner workings of the organization well enough to care. So after six, eight, ten or more months of soliciting feedback, the new structure is approved.

This process seems to happen everywhere. But why do many organizations put so much time, energy and effort into the loud minority of the extremes?

Ask yourself, is change going to:

1. Positively impact the bottom line (and you can prove it)?
2. Make the job functions of volunteers easier?
3. Provide higher value to the membership?

If so, then I say ask for forgiveness and spend much less time asking for permission. I realize this is easier said than done with bylaw changes, etc., but I think we spend way more time in the approval process of change than we do implementing it.

Searching for Your Association's Core Competency?

DAVID GAMMEL

Associations have long built their value to members on creating information products. Conferences, magazines, journals, newsletters and websites all have been traditional vehicles for creating and providing information and knowledge to members that couldn't be had elsewhere.

Then the Web came along. Suddenly, we all have access to vast collections of information. However, this has brought a new challenge—finding the valuable stuff in that massive pile of information. Your association can continue to provide value in an information-rich economy by developing the capacity to assist your members in sifting through it. Invest in understanding how search technology works and how it can be tailored for your members. Think like an information concierge rather than a publisher.

Make helping your members find critical information and knowledge a key part of your value, whether or not you published that information in the first place.

Why Innovation?

JEFF DE CAGNA

I am sometimes asked why associations need to bother with innovation. The answer should be apparent to anyone paying attention to what is happening in the world right now: **Innovation is the most critical capability for associations to develop today to maximize their opportunities for success tomorrow.** The powerful forces of demographic, economic, scientific, social, political and technological shift are converging and forging an entirely new society. The acute challenges this paradigm shift is already creating for associations demands that leaders in our community get serious about thinking, acting and learning like true innovators right away.

So here are five key points you will want to consider as you go about the work of building a genuine commitment to innovation in your association:

- **Creating a culture of innovation is all about unleashing the passion of staff and volunteers.** Growth depends on innovation, and innovation depends entirely on the deep engagement of those who are going to make it happen. Passionate people innovate freely because they know that what they bring to the table is valued. They understand that their leaders view risk as a part of doing business in a time of paradigm shift. When passion takes root in an organization, it makes the possible real, the difficult achievable, and the impossible possible. It is precisely this depth of individual and collective commitment that our organizations will need in the years ahead.
- **Creating an effective innovation culture is a shared responsibility.** Association CEOs play the central role in creating an effective inno-

vation culture, but they cannot do it alone. Association staff and volunteers must work together to create a sustainable culture of experimentation, collaboration and learning. Innovation is an inherently social, highly-networked, and democratic process; everyone has a role to play in making it happen. And anyone can infect the innovation effort with cynicism and skepticism through his or her naysaying behaviors. It is essential, therefore, for innovation leaders to prevent that infection from spreading throughout the organization.

- **An effective innovation culture is all about finding the right balance of freedom and discipline.** For innovation to flourish, there must be both freedom and discipline. On the one hand, innovators must have the freedom to imagine what is possible, develop their ideas collaboratively, and experiment with them in the marketplace. At the same time, the organization must have the requisite discipline to choose only the best ideas, to invest consistently in them and to quickly fail ideas that do not demonstrate potential, while acting on those with the greatest promise. Freedom and discipline are a duality. Discipline in some areas creates the opportunity for freedom in others, and genuine freedom recognizes the constant need for discipline to prevent creativity from descending into chaos. Association leaders must strive at all times to find the right balance of freedom and discipline to provide support for both.

- **Creating an effective innovation culture is not enough to make innovation happen.** Creating an innovation culture is an important step in any association's journey toward the full embrace of innovation as a strategic priority. Unfortunately, culture by itself is not enough. Every association needs a highly transparent and accessible innovation process that is easily understood by all stakeholders. Every association needs to channel a consistent flow of investment resources to the innovation effort and fully engage its whole organization in the challenging work of taking ideas from concept to cash. Traditional notions of innovation being exclusively about products must give way to a broader recognition of innovation as a holistic approach that touches every aspect of the organization's work. While the culture of innovation definitely will facilitate your association's innovation efforts, a set of deeper organizational capabilities is necessary to bring them to fruition.

- **It is the CEO's responsibility to make the case for innovation to the board.** Association CEOs must accept the fundamental responsibility of making the case for innovation to volunteer boards of directors. There is no one else who can do it. The role of any chief executive officer is to ensure the long-term sustainability of the association as an enterprise that creates value for members and customers in a manner consistent with its mission. CEOs, therefore, must directly challenge their boards to accept the core belief that growth depends on innovation. Without growth, there can be no success.

For tradition-bound boards, paralyzed by nostalgia, myopia and intransigence, this will be an unpopular message that may well fall on deaf ears. For boards willing to hear difficult truths, this will be a clarion call to action. Either way, a choice for the future must be made. *What kind of future will your association choose for itself?*

Devaluing Learning by Mandating Continuing Education

MICKIE ROPS

I had an encounter with an individual over a decade ago that made a lasting impression. I was describing to her a tool that would assist her in objectively determining her learning needs, developing a learning plan and guiding her to appropriate learning resources in her area of practice. After agreeing that the tool seemed valuable, she indicated that perhaps she would buy it next year when she starts a new recertification cycle because she didn't need any more hours this cycle. What? Rather than spend $65 (less than the cost of a new pair of shoes!) on a learning tool that could help prioritize her learning pursuits and locate relevant learning activities, she declined, because she had already fulfilled her required learning quota.

Unfortunately, this isn't an isolated incident. **For many fields with certification, the accompanying mandated continuing education (MCE) has devalued learning.** The effects are widespread. The negative ramifications of MCE can be found throughout adult learning literature. Here are just a few.

One concern is relevancy. Professionals become overly concerned with getting their hours. Because usually only the traditional education delivery modes are acceptable (conferences as the most common example), they are essentially **forced to participate in activities that are convenient or affordable but sometimes irrelevant** to their needs.

Another concern is that MCE **devalues many types of learning**, especially those that are more informal and self-directed. Since reading, receiving mentoring or conferring with colleagues, for example, are not usually deemed acceptable learning activities under an MCE system, individuals may question the value of these approaches and assume the traditional approaches are better.

Another criticism of MCE is that it creates **a punitive attitude towards learning**. For those professionals who would regularly engage in learning with or without the mandate, MCE becomes punitive in that it places sanctions on activities that are already occurring. And, for many, it forces them to participate in activities they otherwise wouldn't simply to meet the requirement.

Am I suggesting we scrap all mandated CE? No. But the systems need to change. For one, we should eliminate or at least lessen the excessive judgmental and limiting rules of MCE. Before creating any rule (e.g., deeming some learning methods acceptable and others not, limiting amount of time spent in one type of activity, requiring participation in certain types of activities, etc.), **ask yourself whether this rule helps or actually hinders learning?**

The bottom line: we want certificants to be competent. To be competent, they must engage in continuous learning. But the truth is that we cannot mandate that someone learns. And it's time we realized that requiring "butts in seats" at our conferences is a limited and ineffective approach. **A far more effective approach is to make a concerted effort to foster the value of continuous learning and to provide tools and guidance to professionals to help them be more effective learners.**

Trying to Please Everyone

Jamie Notter

As membership-based organizations, associations by definition must create themselves in a way that allows them to satisfy a large number of stakeholders. Within their membership alone they are guaranteed to find a broad range of preferences and priorities. That range only expands when you consider other stakeholders (business partners, staff, policy communities, the public, etc.). Obviously there is value in creating a variety of experiences, products, services, etc. so that your differing stakeholders can extract different types of value.

For example, AARP produces a very successful magazine. A few years back they experimented with two versions of the magazine, including a new one focused on a specific generation—the newest retirees, the "Baby Boomers." As they evaluated the success of the new venture, however, the results were disappointing, and they cancelled the generation-specific publication. But they did not go back to one magazine for all of their membership. They started producing three slightly different versions of their magazine based on age groupings rather than generations: one for members in their fifties, one for members in their sixties, and one for members seventy and above. This approach has been more successful.

So shifting in response to diversity among stakeholders can be a good thing. But it also has its dark side, and associations too often fail to see this. The dark side lies in the fact that if we try to be everything to everyone, we quite obviously spread resources too thin and end up failing nearly everyone. At a high level, association executives see this and often state publicly that pleasing everyone is impossible.

But move down into implementation and that high level commitment breaks down. The problem is rooted in two contradictory values: responding to member needs and succeeding through strategic choice. We know that providing value to members will make our association successful, so we invest heavily in researching what they value. The more sophisticated we get with our research, the larger the variety of interests we discover. We use that knowledge to tweak our services or processes and we get good results (retention up! satisfaction up!). So we keep doing it.

Unfortunately, over time, this logical process takes us away from strategy. Although we acknowledge that we cannot meet everyone's needs, we still research everyone's needs and set ourselves up for failure. Rather than fail, we end up abandoning strategy. It happens over time. No one makes the explicit decision that making clear strategic choices is bad, but that is what happens.

We must reintroduce the power of choice. You must take some people's interests and desires and give them a higher priority than others. You have to make some people unhappy with your decisions, because if you don't, then you are making weak decisions, and success requires strength. You have to choose some courses of action knowing that you are ruling out a host of other options. You don't have to be blind to what others want, and we don't encourage you to ignore stakeholder groups and their varied interests and opinions. **But you do have to choose.**

Vision and Venture

Jeff De Cagna

I have a great fondness for the inherent power of quotations, and one of my all-time favorites comes from Vaclav Havel, the former president of the Czech Republic:

> *"Vision is not enough; it must be combined with venture. It is not enough to stare up the steps; we must step up the stairs."*

Most associations in which I've been involved in one way or another do a good enough job articulating grand statements of vision and mission. They are less good, however, at venturing something real and meaningful to help make those intentions come true. And yet, as Havel's words confirm, we will never accomplish anything of enduring consequence unless we are prepared to put something at risk in the process. Throughout human history, understanding, accepting and capitalizing on risk has been an element of every meaningful achievement ever attempted. It's time for association staff and volunteer leaders to recognize this inescapable fact.

Of course, by venture, I don't mean the reckless and uninformed pursuit of just any opportunity that may present itself. Venture must be a strategic endeavor, guided by a clear sense of both realism and possibility. Risk is something to be managed and, if possible, leveraged to the benefit of the organization and its members. It can be done, but only if leaders are willing to challenge their associations—and themselves—to "step up the stairs."

Think Like an Entrepreneur First, Like an Association Executive Second

Amy Smith

Dan Sullivan, founder and president of The Strategic Coach, Inc., writes an eNewsletter that is fantastic (www.strategiccoach.com). His organization provides a structured coaching program for entrepreneurs, and his newsletter focuses on specific aspects of the program.

The July 2006 newsletter, *Strategic eNews*, has an article entitled, "Thinking Like an Intellectual Capitalist." Sullivan suggests, "Instead of identifying yourself by the products you sell or the title your industry gives you, you define yourself as an entrepreneur with a specialty in a particular area."

What kinds of mental shifts do you think would happen if association executives changed their mindset to think first like an entrepreneur, then second as an association executive?

Sullivan continues, "This shift allows you to come up with creative responses to others' needs—opening you up to the possibility of doing anything that will create value, not simply acting as a channel for industry goods and services. It also allows you to shift your focus to your biggest asset—your existing relationships."

What a brilliant concept!

We Need a Master's Degree

Jeff De Cagna

The association community needs a credible advanced degree that offers association professionals an educational pathway other than the Certified Association Executive (CAE) designation. An even more important reason to create such a degree program is the dearth of executive-level learning and development that actually helps association leaders operate effectively in a time of profound, accelerating and intensifying disruption and discontinuity. Let me put it another way: **There is good reason to question whether today's association leaders are adequately prepared to deal with the realities of the genuine paradigm shift that is already taking place in our society.** Can we really afford to do nothing to address this issue?

To initiate a dialogue on this topic, let me offer the following specific thoughts about how I would design an Executive Master of Science in Association Leadership (EMSAL) degree program:

- EMSAL would be a twenty-month, cohort-based program organized into five, four-month learning modules with intensive course sessions conducted once per month on Friday and Saturday.
- Each cohort would include no more than twenty-five participants, but multiple cohorts could be in the program at once, with groups entering in September, January and May if necessary.
- During each module, cohort members would be organized into five different project teams, so that each participant would have the opportunity to collaborate with everyone else in the cohort. Each module would conclude with a team project.
- The five module topics would be: (1) The Historical Evolution of Associations, (2) The Role of Associations in a Global Society, (3) The Role of Associations in Industry and the Professions, (4) The Role of the Individual in Associations, and (5) Leadership of Associations in the 21st century.
- The global society module would include a study mission of some length (perhaps ten to fourteen days) outside of North America.

- The course curriculum would be multidisciplinary, drawing on a variety of fields including anthropology, business and management, economics, education, future studies, history, leadership, natural and physical sciences, political science, psychology, sociology and technology.
- Both individual and team assessment would be a part of determining whether a participant successfully completes the program, including individual learning portfolios, peer evaluations and team projects.
- Learning facilitation would be conducted by both faculty from the university partner and senior leaders in the association community.

I realize this is an ambitious program design, and that is entirely intentional. Some in our community appear to believe that what we do in associations isn't important enough to merit the most forward-looking and intensive learning and leadership development opportunity possible.

I strenuously disagree.

We need to give association leaders today and tomorrow every opportunity to build their understanding of the forces of paradigm shift so they can elevate the quality of their leadership going forward. We have a deep responsibility to these leaders, their organizations and members, the professions, industries and fields their associations serve and to society as whole to make this kind of innovation a priority. I hope we soon will be prepared to act on making it a reality.

The Holy Grail of Great Ideas

Mickie Rops

I can have a great idea, and you can have a great idea, but is my idea going to be great for you and yours great for me? (If you can follow that sentence, you're approved to read on.)

Next time you're at a conference, when a speaker starts presenting their "great ideas" for how to do something, notice how many people around the room are ferociously scribbling down all the ideas. This is when I get a little uncomfortable. The sharing of ideas is great—if I'm there, I'll probably be scribbling the ideas down too. What concerns me is that presenters often advocate their ideas as golden rules, and what concerns me more is that many participants seem to buy what the presenters are selling.

We need to be clear that just because one person's "great idea" was proven successful for a particular situation, that's little to no indication for how it will play out for another organization. An analogy for all you parents out there: Did all those great ideas you collected for handling your first child work identically for all your children?! How about those great ideas you were offered from other parents with swears of success—did they all work for you?

We all need to recognize that **any idea we hear, no matter how successful it was in a given situation, is only a "potentially great idea" to us** (a PGI, that is, because the association world needs a few more acronyms). It's up to us to determine what the potential success of that idea will be in our particular situation.

Hmmm, do you think ASAE & the Center for Association Leadership will rename their conference the "Potentially Great Ideas Conference?" Okay, maybe not.

CHANGING THE WAY WE LEAD

Strategy and Planning Are Not the Same

JAMIE NOTTER

The association community is almost obsessed with strategic planning. Although more room is now being given to the dissenting opinion that perhaps the way we have always done strategic planning is no longer serving us, there are still many out there who stand unquestioningly behind their two-day retreats, their SWOT analyses, and their thirty-nine-page, three-ring-bound strategic plans that effectively become "credenza-ware" for the next two to three years.

There are many problems with traditional strategic planning, and we address several in this book. One critical problem is literally the combination of those two words—strategic and planning. Everyone agrees that associations need strategy. Without a clear strategy, associations can only be reactive, and that is unlikely to generate long-term success. A strategy exists to guide proactive decision-making and should reflect careful thinking about how and why the association will succeed.

Organizations also need planning. It's not enough simply to know where you are headed. If you ignore the details of how you are going to get there, then you are likely to end up in a significantly different place, or at the right place, but at the wrong time.

But combining strategy and planning (as is done in traditional strategic planning) is very dangerous, because strategy and planning are very different things. The strategy is incredibly important and relatively stable and constant. It should take a significant amount of information and conversation to produce a strategic change. Planning, on the other hand, does not have that weight. It is a means to an end, and should be much more flexible. But when we combine strategy and plan, we end up adding the weight of the strategy to the plan. This creates dangerous inflexibility.

Consultant and author Jeffrey Pfeffer recently wrote about a CEO who was heading toward failure because he had "convinced himself that his strategy was the only way to go." As Pfeffer said, "if you become so attached to your course of action that proving it right becomes more important than your overall success, chances are you are not going to succeed." (*Business 2.0*, November 2005)

When plans are too tightly linked to the strategy, they actually invite blind commitment ("But it's part of the strategic plan—we can't change that!"). Of course your planning process should involve an awareness of and discussion of the strategy. But there needs to be some distance, so everyone will be clear about when they are making a strategic move versus when they are modifying a means to an end. The trick is to think and act strategically while modifying your plans. To do that we recommend simply, but powerfully, changing your language. Talk about strategy. Talk about planning. But do not talk about (or do) strategic planning.

Outcomes Orientation for Everyone

DAVID GAMMEL

All units in your association should be focused on achieving your overall outcomes. I don't care what they do. Everyone should be talking about how to achieve them.

Let's illustrate this with an example: growing annual meeting attendance by twenty percent. What could HR do to contribute to this outcome? Re-writing the employee handbook certainly won't help. But what if HR began talking with the meetings department and helped them tailor their position descriptions to better focus on marketing the conference? What if they helped the VP of Meetings design and implement effective incentives programs for growing meeting attendance? What if they proactively searched out candidates who had great experience in growing meeting attendance? You get the idea.

Of course, this requires identifying your outcomes in the first place. That is where your senior executives need to put their attention: identifying the organization's outcomes and then getting everyone talking about how they can contribute to achieving them.

No More Excuses

JEFF DE CAGNA

Leaders, and I mean *real* leaders, **do not** make excuses. Real leaders take responsibility for whatever is going on in the organization—good or bad—regardless of whether they are actually responsible for creating those circumstances. Real leaders recognize that today's success, no matter how robust it may be, eventually *will* run out of steam. After all, no organization thrives in perpetuity, yet complacency is a rather common and extremely deadly affliction of the successful enterprise. On the flip side, real leaders recognize that today's decline *will* get worse if intelligent decisions are not made in an effort to reverse the trend. Real leaders think clearly about what *is*, while also thinking creatively about what *is possible*. Real leaders don't wait for conditions to irrevocably deteriorate before taking some form of action, even if that action involves risk.

So here is my question: **Does your association have *real* leaders?**

I know that posing such a direct and difficult question will raise the ire of some in our community. To be honest with you, however, we can't worry about that. If there is anything we really have to change about associations, it is the absolutely cavernous leadership gap. From my perspective, while we definitely must address significant shortcomings in the way association staff leaders are prepared for their roles, the bigger challenge for the community is with our volunteers. Throughout my career, I have been witness to extraordinary shortsightedness on the part of volunteer leaders who really should know better. In recent years, as the work of associations has become more complex and volunteers have become busier, the problem appears to have become more acute. **How much longer will our community endure this myopia?**

It is important that we not treat this as merely a rhetorical question. The association community must develop a next generation of staff and volunteer leaders who do not need to be persuaded to the belief that renewed success will be achieved only through a radical shift in how we do our work. That shift is already happening all around us. We must accelerate our efforts before we're lagging too far behind to catch up.

Presidential Agendas Be Gone

Mickie Rops

I'll never forget a conversation I had with a past president of an association. She recalled her first meeting with the association CEO who asked her what her agenda would be for the upcoming year. The president was confused. "My agenda?" she asked. "My agenda is to meet the strategic objectives of the association." Ah, how refreshing...and dare I say rare? I sometimes wonder how some associations get anything done, much less the right things done, with this revolving door of leaders and priorities.

Do the priorities of your association change with the annual install-ment of new officers? Now, honestly ask yourself: Do you in any way encourage this ridiculous presidential rite? Consider the scenario described earlier. That CEO started out each year asking the president what his or her agenda was going to be. Talk about handing it to him or her on a silver platter! Even if the president didn't have an agenda before, he or she probably would create one.

What type of initial conversation do you have with your incoming leaders? What a difference could be made by starting out with a dis-cussion of the association's current strategic priorities and asking what particular ideas the president has to move these forward. And, notice I said ideas, not mandates. The ideas leaders have should always be scrutinized to the same extent as any potential project or program idea.

Volunteer leaders want to make their mark. To be fair, given their ded-ication, they probably deserve it. **But association CEOs need to estab-lish a culture in which the leaders understand that the appropriate way to make their mark is to advance the association, its members, and the field it represents, not their own personal agendas.**

Do Three Things

Davdi Gammel

When your organization has no discernible strategy, what can you do? Make up your own!

Don't let a lack of strategic direction or guidance from your leadership stop you. If you have been on staff for much time, you have a good idea of where the organization is going in the short term, even if your leadership is not capable of expressing it. Identify a few goals for your organization, unit or self based on what you know about the associa-tion. This shouldn't be hard to do. Next, identify three things you can do this week to move along towards achieving those goals. Then do them. Pretty simple, huh?

If you continue to do three things each week for those goals, you will be surprised how much progress you will make without relying on leadership from above. (By the way, you are leading when you do this, whether you realize it or not!) Taking some focused action in the short term is almost always better than freezing like a deer in the headlights. Get out there and do three things!

Financial Acumen

AMY SMITH

You cannot assume that staff members know, understand or care about your organization's financial information and metrics. All too often individuals are promoted to positions with little knowledge of basic financial terminology or, more importantly, what it means for their work.

Why is financial acumen important to everyone in the organization? You may find that by providing some basic financial training, your staff, and subsequently the organization, may perform better. People can feel a stronger sense of ownership when they understand and can be held accountable to the bottom line for a program, campaign, etc.

Investing in the financial education of your staff at all levels can help ensure better financial success. It also provides a great accountability tool for all staff members and gives them a greater sense of value to the organization.

Avoiding Disruptions

JAMIE NOTTER

There was a quote in the winter 2006 *Journal of Association Leadership* that reflects a fundamental stumbling block in the association community. In the commentary to an article about strategy making, Adrienne Bien expressed concern about the resistance the author encountered when bringing a new approach to strategy to his association:

> *For most associations, this resistance would be a red flag, as we tend to avoid conflict and steer away from disruptions to the volunteer structures that are the backbones of our organizations.*

Forget just the volunteer structures; associations steer away from disruption. We want things to go smoothly. We want things to go as we planned them. We want the activities of the association to unfold predictably, resulting in universal acclaim and positive feedback.

Unfortunately, that is fantasy. In real life there are disruptions. We can certainly plan and strive to do things that people find valuable (it is okay to score "fives" on your evaluation sheets). As life unfolds, however, we are bound to find disruptions. People don't show up. The program is not making participants happy. The staff does not like the new initiative we just announced.

At that moment, you need to embrace the disruption, rather than avoid it. Disruptions are infinitely more valuable than your stack of "happy sheets" with all fives on them. They open your eyes to new possibilities and support you in confronting the truth. Without disruptions, you would continue to do what you've always done—even if it isn't working.

Avoiding or ignoring disruptions is certainly tempting. At the first sign you can look the other way, silence the disruptive voices, or even stop asking questions, in order to avoid disruptive answers. That feels more comfortable, because it allows you to focus on the positive messages and feel good about the way things are going.

Resist the temptation. Ask yourself which is more important: comfort or success? Your chances for success increase proportionally with the amount of information you let in, and by avoiding disruptions you close off a critical channel of information, resulting in missed opportunities for growth and change. The next time you have a disruption—even one in your volunteer structure—move towards it instead of away from it. Learn more about it. Ask questions. Dig deeper. The decisions that emerge will be smarter.

The Absolute Necessity of Ethics and Social Responsibility

Jeff De Cagna

It has been said that ethics is the choice to do the right thing even when no one is watching. In other words, ethical people and organizations act that way because they are deeply committed to doing what is proper *at all times*, not simply when such behavior is expedient. The current turbulent operating environment, in which strategic decisions increasingly are made under conditions of incomplete information, limited time and considerable stress, demands that association leaders take a long, hard look at both their personal and organizational ethics and ask some fundamental questions:

• Do I consider the implications of my actions/my organization's actions for others?
• Do both my organization and I pursue the ethical path at all times?
• Is my integrity and the integrity of my organization intact?

Although framed as clear choices, these questions defy simple yes or no answers. Their intention is to help association leaders surface the underlying decision-making principles that enable consistent ethical conduct in the short term, as well as the creation of an organizational legacy of honesty, integrity and social responsibility that will endure in the long run. Sadly, there are far too many recent examples from both corporate and social enterprises of the kind of irresponsible, unethical and outright corrupt behavior that undermines the public's trust and confidence in all institutions, including associations. Associations and their leaders will not get a pass from intense scrutiny of their conduct. If the failure to act in an ethical and responsible manner erodes support among our constituents for the important work that our organizations perform, it may irreparably compromise the historic role of associations in American society.

Meaningful conversations about ethics and social responsibility are not likely to be at the top of the agenda for many association leaders. We are fortunate, however, that these questions are increasingly a part of our community's dialogue, not as a matter of choice, but of necessity. But simply talking about these issues won't be sufficient; decisive action is required. The best association leaders of the 21st century already understand that a vibrant and sustainable future for associations depends, in part, on our community's unswerving commitment to and full-throated public advocacy for ethics and social responsibility across our society. Anything less would be a retreat from the core beliefs that make our organizations great.

Do You Know What Your Members Know?

Mickie Rops

Many associations have identified the body of knowledge of the fields they represent and used them for specific purposes, such as developing training or certification programs. However, often the body of knowledge is used only for that specific and independent purpose. And associations may have even identified several different bodies of knowledge for unrelated projects. As a typical example, the professional development division creates a knowledge matrix for tracking its curriculum, the certification division formally identifies a body of knowledge for its certification examination, the publications division compiles a topical index for its books and magazines, and the communications division identifies an index for its Web portal. All are created at different times, using different methods, by different units, for different purposes. These often informal and unplanned knowledge efforts can be valuable to the association and its members. **But they could have much more impact if they were coordinated as part of an association's overall knowledge strategy.**

If you haven't identified the current body of knowledge of the field in which your members work (or a portion of that field), consider:

- How do you determine what knowledge and skills are currently and will be needed by your members in the next 5 years?
- How do you determine what to teach members in your educational programs?
- What do you use as your basis for selecting content for your publications?
- How do you prioritize research efforts to advance the field? (How do you advance a field if you don't know its current status?)
- What is the foundation of your certification program examination?

It's time for associations to get strategic and purposeful about how they will advance the knowledge of their members and/or advance the fields in which their members work. Identifying the body of knowledge can be an important first step. It may (but does not have to) be an elaborate research project. How sophisticated the approach is depends upon the identified uses for that body of knowledge. Certification, for example, does warrant a sophisticated approach—usually a formal job analysis. However, if you are trying to identify the gap between what members currently know and what they'll need to know in five years (so that you can be purposeful in getting your members there!), qualitative research of key employers may do the job fine. So that takes us back to strategy. Associations need to identify what their knowledge goals are first and then identify the strategies and action plans to get there.

Still questioning the value of a knowledge strategy? The Project Management Institute has been purposeful in its knowledge efforts, and it has paid off. Its *Guide to the Project Management Body of Knowledge™* book is currently on the *BusinessWeek* Best Seller List!

Membership Should Be More than a Discount

DAVID GAMMEL

How many organizations have you joined in order to get a 5% discount? Not too many, I would guess. However, this kind of benefit is often a huge focus of associations in their membership marketing materials and the affinity partnerships that they develop. If you look back at the origins of most associations, they had no benefits like this at the start. It was association for the sake of associating and wanting to make a difference. We need to make sure we continue to offer meaning behind our memberships.

I recently heard a member of an association state that he wanted the image of his association to make him proud to be a member of both the organization and the profession it represents. Now that is a reason to join! How proud does your organization make your members?

Developing Strategy by Department

JAMIE NOTTER

Yet another component of strategic planning that we feel needs changing is the tendency to structure the planning work by department. When it comes time to do the strategic plan, each department takes stock of its activities and translates them into quantifiable goals for the upcoming year. Predictably, the strategic plan has a section for each department, complete with goals, action plans, and timelines. While it is true that each department will spend time doing different things throughout the year, this approach to strategy has some major flaws.

First, it reinforces the status quo. Updating strategy morphs into merely updating the metrics on a previously devised strategy. The strategy stays the same each year: you do your meetings, your education, your membership activities—it's only a question of how much. This year becomes last year plus three percent. This may generate results in the short run, but this approach removes innovation from the equation. It will certainly fall short over the long term. Like every living system, organizations (and their strategies) must change.

Second, it reinforces those silos that everyone complains about. Each department creates its own goals by itself, so it stands to reason that implementation will be a solitary activity as well. This can actually inhibit cooperation and information sharing. Departments can create priorities that eventually come into conflict, but as you were focusing on your department's goals, you missed the opportunity to resolve the issue early on (when it was easy to resolve). Now it is a crisis. This is typically perceived as the other department letting you down, which creates an even deeper divide between departments.

Third, it inhibits a truly strategic reaction to changes in the operating environment. Sometimes a key strategic issue will emerge that impacts only one department—but that is rare. Strategic issues affect departments differently, but when each department plans and implements independently, you are unable to get a coordinated response. For one department it is a crisis, for another it is a low priority. They do not respond on the same time schedule, slowing the response time for the whole organization.

The solution to this problem lies first and foremost at the top of the organization. The CEO and the heads of each department must create opportunities for cross-program strategy generation and implementation. While there is certainly a portion of the senior manager's attention that focuses exclusively on their department, if they do not devote time to hashing out overall organizational priorities on a regular basis, they will fall into the silo trap. When the senior team can work effectively through cross-program priority setting, they can then manage their own department's priorities and actions more effectively.

Board Members and Recruiting Younger Members

Amy Smith

Here are some thoughts to ponder:

Why would anyone over fifty choose to join an organization if all of the people on the Board were under forty and white women?

What would you think if there was one man on the Board? What if one of the women was a minority? What if one of the Board members was over sixty-five?

Why would anyone under forty choose to join an organization if all of the people on the Board were over fifty and primarily white males?

What would you think if there was one woman on the Board? What if one of the men was a minority? What if one of the Board members was under twenty-five?

A few editorial comments…

I'd argue that any Board consisting of women under forty would never be that homogeneous to begin with—and I can say that because I'm on one. I'd also say that folks from GenX have a much broader sense of community and value the diverse experiences across age, gender, race, ethnicity, etc. We look at that as a strength.

I can also tell you that I have consciously looked at the makeup of corporate Boards whose companies sell products and services to my business. I make buying choices based on this. In this day and age, if your organization is not walking the talk and diversifying the Board to the fullest extent possible, why should I join? Clearly your organization doesn't get it.

So the next time you want to complain about not being able to attract younger folks to your organization, take a look at your Board. Do they truly reflect your membership?

Boards We Cannot Afford

Jeff De Cagna

In an article in the May–June 2006 issue of *Harvard Magazine*, Harvard Graduate School of Education professor Richard Chait makes the following argument about the proper role of boards:

> *When boards operate at their very best, they are able to spot institutional blind spots. They're able to see what management has either chosen to neglect or simply doesn't have the acuity to see.*

When questioned on whether boards actually operate in this way, Chait offers an alternative formulation of his original idea:

> *Let's change from blind spots to exactly the opposite—that boards have to identify what's so obvious that nobody sees it.*

Whether it is blind spots or challenges hidden in plain sight, Chait's perspectives are a breath of fresh air. Too many association boards are so deeply embedded in the machinery of governance that they often fail at what is clearly their primary role: **to develop a sharp and comprehensive vision of the world in which the organization operates— for better or for worse—so they can make more intelligent strategic choices.** If association boards are willing to do this job, the future of their organizations, as well as the professions, industries and fields they serve, should look much brighter.

To help association community boards achieve the very high standard for excellence that Chait sets for them, it is useful also to isolate some of the counterproductive and disconcerting ways of thinking and acting that boards too often adopt and that we simply can no longer accept. We cannot afford boards that:

- Tolerate denial, nostalgia, myopia or intransigence. We need boards that recognize and accept the emerging reality of profound, accelerating and intensifying disruption and discontinuity, i.e., genuine paradigm shift. We need board members who understand the new drivers of growth and success in this uncertain environment.
- Defer difficult choices to the future in the interest of keeping the peace today. We need boards that will confront divisive issues, even if some people might be angered or offended by the result. We need board members who accept the necessity of constructive conflict that serves a larger, strategic purpose.
- Willingly revoke their public commitments in the interest of expedience or political pressure. We need boards with integrity. We need board members who understand that it is more important to stand behind smart decisions than it is to be popular.
- Value the superficial over the substantive. We need boards that deeply embrace their leadership responsibilities, while eschewing the accompanying perquisites. We need board members who embrace the privilege of board service as its own reward.
- Interfere with or prevent the pursuit of innovation. We need boards that are guided by a strategic mindset and imbued with an entrepre-

neurial spirit. We need board members who understand the preeminence of value creation for members, customers and stakeholders.

In short, our associations need and deserve stronger, better boards. Our community can no longer afford to abide boards that don't make building and strengthening their own performance a priority. The long-term success of our community depends, at least in part, on our ability to infuse board leaders with the conviction that while good intentions to do your best are a beginning, they aren't a sufficient basis for doing the hard work of leading our organizations into the future. To do that at the level of excellence suggested by Professor Chait, much more is required.

Fearing Rejection

JAMIE NOTTER

Associations are afraid of rejection. They want to please everyone. They do not want to offer something unless they know that people will show up and will provide universally glowing evaluation forms. The desire to produce high-quality and high-value products and services, of course, is laudable. But it is important to remember that the path to that high-value endpoint will often take you through rejection and frustration. To assume that you can always get it right simply denies our own experience.

Who makes the right decisions all the time? Who accurately predicts what people will want or need with 100% accuracy? The very best hitters in professional baseball fail to get base hits 65% of the time. We learn, grow, and are successful in life by trying and sometimes failing. As long as we learn from what did not work, we make great progress. The more we try, the more we learn, and the more successful we are.

But associations forget this. They are reluctant to experiment. What if the members don't like it? What if we get low scores on the evaluation forms? Two of us were planning a session for a conference with the client and we proposed a format that was non-traditional for this client. They balked. What if people come into the room, see the non-traditional format, and then leave for another session?

Our response: Great! This session is not designed to please everyone. Some may want to go elsewhere, but we think some will like it and want to stay. But we will only know this if we try. We will only learn what works if we risk being rejected.

CHANGING THE WAY WE MANAGE

Get Them Outta Here!

AMY SMITH

While I am a huge fan of Jim Collins, *Good to Great* has been overused in many association circles. However, the book's concept of getting the right people on the bus, the wrong people off, and the right people in the right seats is truly critical to the long-term success of associations and nonprofits.

However, here is a classic always-done-it-that-way item: "Let's keep dead weight staff on board until they retire."

You have to understand that one of my first jobs out of college was working for a very elite management consulting firm, where the average tenure for new hires was about one-and-a-half to two years. You either moved up or out, and there was no other way in that organization. The environment ensured that only the most highly motivated and highest caliber individuals stayed in the organization. This environment created an amazingly high-performing organization, and it was really exciting to work there. The firm took care of its employees and went so far as to pay you to conduct a full-time job search if you were not promoted. What a novel concept!

What is the deal with associations holding on to dead weight staffers and senior managers who are underperforming, toxic to productive employees or, even worse, are just the wrong people on the bus? I wonder what people are thinking by keeping these folks on board? Really, think about it. Competition is heating up, productivity is critical and no one has time to deal with the toxicity of employees that need to find new work. Why do we as an industry not place more value on getting the wrong people off of the bus? Productivity is critical, and I do not mean simply cranking out the same old stuff, but creating new, exciting, highly valued products and services for members.

On a similar note, why are the same people doing the same job for fifteen, twenty or more years? I would suggest that if the same person has been doing the same job for that long, it is time for a change, both for the organization and the individual. Now keep in mind, I did not say fire that person if they are productive, but help them find a new seat on the bus.

And for everyone's sake, get rid of those who do not belong on the bus!

Staff Meetings

Jamie Notter

When is the last time you heard anyone in your association say, "Oh boy, it's time for staff meeting!" In fact, most people hate staff meetings. But for some reason we treat it like going to the dentist—we hate being there, but we know we're better off in the long term by going.

It doesn't have to be that way (at least for staff meetings). It is true that staff meetings serve a purpose in the long term. We need to be aware of what others in the organization are doing, and we need to know how what we are doing connects to the organization's strategy.

But staff meetings need not be painful and boring. In fact, with the pressures on association staff to do more with less, we really cannot afford to spend as many as two hours per week wasting time. We need new solutions that allow staff to communicate and act strategically, without boring them to tears.

For example, you can make staff meetings more engaging and focused by distinguishing between big-picture discussions of strategy from the simpler sharing of implementation details. Patrick Lencioni, in his book, Death by Meeting, recommends that "strategic meetings" occur only monthly, cover one or two topics, and require staff to do homework and intense preparation before they convene. In the weekly tactical staff meetings, however, the agenda is created mid-way through the meeting, based on issues identified in the initial go-round. By creating a clearer context for discussion, the meetings can actually be more engaging and productive.

There are also ways to leverage technology in solving this problem. What about creating an internal staff meeting blog? Individuals or department heads can post reports on what they are doing. Other staff can comment with questions and get responses to areas that are specifically relevant to them, skipping over the parts that are not as important. And people can do this on their own time during the week. This way when you do actually convene a meeting, people have more information when they start, and the conversation is more focused and effective.

Those are simply two ideas for changing the way you do staff meetings. You will have to experiment with alternatives. Try them out for at least a month or two then evaluate their effectiveness as a staff. When people are genuinely excited about coming to the meetings, you will know you have it right.

Can We Make It the 45% Rule Instead?

Jeff De Cagna

The rule of thumb in our community is that an association should have an amount in reserves equal to 50% of its budget, just in case the organization's financial position begins to deteriorate. So, for example, if I am the CEO of a $10 million association, I'm looking to accumulate $5 million in my reserve fund as expeditiously as possible. It makes complete sense, right?

Of course it does, and that's why I can't resist mucking things up by proposing a minor edit: **Let's make it 45% instead.** And let's invest the other 5% in the work of innovation for the future. After all, it's a rule of thumb, not a requirement, regulation or law, so we can make it whatever we want it to be. And just imagine the extraordinary impact that 5% of your reserves would have on the pursuit of innovation in the community your association serves!

There are great reasons to pursue this alternative. First and foremost, by investing 5% in innovation, you will be making a powerful and appropriate statement that you value the creativity, energy and passion of the people who make up your association more than financial markets. Second, building a deep capacity for innovation creates tangible and intangible benefits for your association—new ideas, new capabilities, brand equity, member engagement and new revenue streams—that will never come about from even the most successful portfolio of investments. And finally, if your innovation efforts produce a winner, the financial upside to your future reserve fund investments could be quite considerable. Surely these attractive opportunities are worth an investment of 5%?

Well, I know what you're going to say. "we don't like to take risks." **So, you don't think you're taking risks in the market?** Yes, I know you're carefully managing your portfolio and doing the other stuff all smart investors do, but that isn't the point. Risk is an element of today's operating environment and present in every choice that leaders make. No amount of careful planning, smart implementation or wishful thinking will eliminate it altogether, nor do we want to eliminate it. Wouldn't it be incredibly boring and routine to run an organization in an environment of zero risk? What would be the point? **The issue isn't whether your organization likes to take risks, but how much risk you're willing to accept.** And if you're investing any of your reserves in the market, you've already decided that you will tolerate at least some degree of risk in exchange for a certain level of reward.

Unfortunately, you exercise absolutely no control over the rewards the market will bring you. But you do have levers you can pull when it comes to innovation. By taking a strategic approach to innovation, your organization can invest its 5% in ways that minimize and manage risk by limiting uncertainty and controlling financial exposure, while maximizing whatever upside a given idea may produce. You can't get away from risk, so it is critical that you take steps to make it work for you. The pursuit of innovation in a systemic way should be one of those steps.

I'm thinking, therefore, that just about every organization in our community could make do with 45% in reserves instead of 50%. I'm also thinking that, in the long run, if your association allocates 5% of reserves to the work of innovation, it will turn out to be one of the most beneficial investments the organization has ever made.

Incremental Improvements Rather than Massive Redesigns

DAVID GAMMEL

Massive website redesigns are often very disruptive. Significant changes to navigation and overall design will confuse your current users who knew how to work with the old site, no matter how unfriendly it may have been. How can you improve the site without creating this disruption?

Instead of waiting for a big redesign to make changes, look at making small, incremental changes every week that each improve the site a small amount. Over time, these will add up to a significant difference. Additionally, the change will be gradual so that your visitors can adjust to the changes easily as they happen, avoiding a big disruption.

For example, Yahoo! has added new options to their home page frequently throughout the years. Each addition was just a small change, but the change from a few years ago compared to today is jarring.

The Wild Goose Chase

AMY SMITH

Another title could be, "Where are the Executive Director and/or the President of the Board?"

An artful relationship exists between an association's executive director and the president of the board of directors, with one representing the staff side and the other representing the profession or industry. However, occasionally one has to wonder what either party is doing when volunteers send staff on wild goose chases. Better yet, one of these two parties sends staff on random assignments, wasting staff resources on pet projects.

Wondering what I am referring to? These are the random requests made by volunteer leaders for association staff time and resources. These requests often include things outside the scope of the primary purpose of the organization, or the tasks or assignments have not been thought through, but eat away at staff time.

I witnessed just this kind of activity while in a volunteer role. Six staff members spent an entire day putting together token gifts for new members. The idea, while not bad, was never thought out and was completely last minute. However, what was most surprising was that the executive director did not step in to set some expectations for the project—or better yet, outsource it to a fulfillment house. After some inquiry, staff members told me that this is typical in this volunteer-driven organization. I was shocked. It made me wonder where the board president was and why the president was not reigning in the volunteer leaders. In addition, why did the staff feel compelled to say "yes" to every project that was thrown at them? Moreover, where was the executive director in all of this?

I am wondering how many other organizations have similar situations? I think many organizations have never been truly bottom-line focused and therefore do not seem to value how staff account for their time. Executive directors and presidents may want to periodically examine the path in which new projects enter the staff pipeline.

Complaining About Silos

Jamie Notter

Every association divides its work into departments. This is not unique to associations, of course, but associations seem particularly good at it. There are associations with less than ten staff people that are able to maintain six or seven departments! Division of labor is a rational thing to do, of course, and the department structure is not evil, but it does tend to generate a serious morale-buster—silo wars.

Even with one- and two-person departments, you will find people complaining about how the other departments are not pulling their weight, are getting too much of the budget, lack professionalism, etc. Nearly everyone complains about the other departments, and the complaints come from every level in the hierarchy. People waste time complaining about the silos, and they often end up constricting information flow because of unnecessary competitiveness. We're all on the same team, people. Why can't we just get along?

Unfortunately, it is not just about getting along. No matter how strongly you urge your employees to cooperate and work cross-functionally, if you don't take care of some important issues at the top of your organization, the silo wars will continue. It sounds counterintuitive, but working on issues among the senior management team is the best way to get the complaining at the staff level to stop. There are three key areas that require attention, all of which are areas that associations typically undervalue.

Focus your strategy

Silos will cooperate when they get clear messages about priorities. Association strategic plans typically break down by department, allowing each department to focus on their own goals, but also generating unending debates about whose goals are more important. All departments have importance, but your strategy still must have a focused rallying cry to guide the short- to medium-term. Everyone may be important, but right now we're focusing on [fill in the blank]. When that is communicated clearly and consistently, people will more readily work together towards that goal.

Tighten your senior team

You must include accountability around silo competitiveness as a component of senior team effectiveness. Many associations do not. They overemphasize technical expertise (after all, government relations and meeting planning are fundamentally different things), allowing Vice Presidents to focus primarily on their own department. Issues of competition between departments then become personal (which means they are ignored and fester). This dynamic needs to be nipped in the bud. Issues that generate competition need to be identified and resolved quickly and visibly at the very top of the organization. Without that behavior modeled, it will be too easy to start a campaign of justified complaining at the lower levels. When members of the senior team fail to do this, there must be consequences.

Make the time to do things together

You do not have to restructure into a "matrix" organization or send your people to an off-site to get them to work more cross-functionally. What they need most is a better understanding of what the other departments *really* do. To learn that, they need to spend time with their colleagues in other departments, working with them, talking to them, and asking questions. This takes them away from their own work, and that is perfectly fine. The time you save in inter-departmental cooperation will more than make up for it. But the leadership must support this time investment and manage workflow accordingly. That might even involve modifying deadlines within your own department, if necessary. You must demonstrate your commitment to supporting cross-department cooperation if that is what you really want.

Disempowered Staff Leads to Lousy Member Service

MICKIE ROPS

How many times a day do your staff members say no to members or potential members? Can you fax me a receipt? No. Can I pay for that by purchase order? No. Can you express deliver that if I give you my account number? No. Can I substitute x for y in the product package? No. Are these interactions pleasing members? No. In most cases, would there be any harm in saying yes to these requests? NO! Often association staff members have been given general policies or rules and have been given no authority to make exceptions in the cases where they don't make sense or would cause no harm.

Here's an example. An association has a general policy stating that guests are not permitted at educational events. The rationale for the policy is that many of the events are sold-out and there is no room to accommodate unpaid guests (who are usually spouses or kids) without negative impact on the paid attendees. During check-in for a workshop, a participant asks if her niece, a college student in the association's field, could attend the first session since she is graduating soon, will be eligible for membership in the association, and thought it would be interesting to see what the organization is like. Despite the obvious low attendance at this workshop and numerous open seats, the staff person follows the policy and tells the member and *potential member* that no guests are allowed. The member enters the workshop with a sigh; the *likely no longer a potential member* leaves with a smirk.

Ouch. If you had been there, you would have made an exception, we're sure. But you can't always be there. So **have you empowered your staff to make exceptions to general policies/office rules, when warranted?** Dick Brown, chairman and CEO of EDS, says it best: "Chalk out the playing field and say, within those lines, make any decisions you need." The "chalking out" part is important, though. Strictly following policies and rules usually seems clear, so don't be surprised if you meet with some resistance from staff when you try to explain to them that they can make exceptions (which is unclear). You'll want to invest time in training and providing guidance on when exceptions should or should not be made. Explain the intent behind the policies/rules and discuss potential cases that could arise and desired outcomes. Be clear on when staff do or do not have authority to make exceptions and be clear on whom they should consult with if they need guidance. And perhaps you'll discover you need to changes some of your rules.

Above all, this will require a cultural change in the organization— from one in which "rules are rules" to one in which rules are important, but customers are more important. In this environment, rules should be considered for their appropriateness before applying to any specific situation.

Organizational Dashboard

Amy Smith

There has been so much discussion in popular business publications about the importance of creating a "dashboard." This is a tool that senior executives use to measure performance or results of just about any business-related information you need to know. For you as the Chief Executive of an association or nonprofit, organizational dashboards can provide critical information that can be used to make good business decisions for the association.

I am in the process of creating a dashboard for my organization right now. The process is eye opening and amazingly useful. On a bi-weekly basis I know exactly where I stand on a range of issues and feel like I have a much better way of tracking new initiatives within the organization.

Here are some questions to get you started.

What items should be put on the dashboard? Great question. This is personal to each individual/organization. Initially I looked for articles and/or books on the subject, but I quickly abandoned this because, as a small business owner, I don't have the same metrics that big companies may have.

What performance measures do you have and what are the metrics (financial goals, program measurements, prospective members, reserve amounts, etc.)? You may want to start wherever you need to see change. Add these items to a "change" section of the dashboard. Create a "reality check" and a "target" for each of these items, and list where you are today (reality check) and where you want to be.

What items do you need to know about on a regular basis to make sound business decisions for your organization? Add these items to a "maintenance" section of the dashboard. Some ideas: membership numbers in key categories, the status of major GR issues or status of an IT implementation.

Who should be involved in creating and updating the dashboard? Maybe it is you, maybe it is the senior management team, maybe it is the entire staff. It's your call, but regardless, make sure that the dashboard is useful to you as a management tool. Keep in mind the final use of the tool.

Why is this important? Too many association executives do not think entrepreneurially about their organization. The creation of the dashboard allows you to get, in one place, a great snapshot of exactly what you need to know on a regular basis. It provides a great reality check on where you are and where you are headed.

What If There Were No Dues?

JEFF DE CAGNA

Let's try a thought experiment…

After numerous complaints from members over a three-year period, your board concludes the association's dues are simply too high. The dues are so burdensome, in fact, that they have become the number one reason why even very good prospects don't join. After extensive deliberation and discussion of the issue, the board votes to get rid of dues permanently, even though these payments represent at least 20% (and sometimes more) of your association's revenue each fiscal year.

If confronted with this situation, what would you do differently?

If you don't know, why? If you do, why aren't you already doing it?

Building Teams

JAMIE NOTTER

Anyone managing associations knows that when groups of people work more smoothly together, the organization's results are bound to improve. Everyone agrees that a high-functioning team is a good thing.

The typical response to this challenge, however, is to do team building. This frequently involves bringing the team to an interesting location for a one- or two-day off-site meeting where they can get to know each other better, play some fun games, learn some interesting concepts about trust or communication, and head back to the office refreshed and "built" as a team.

Unfortunately, that is all a lie. While the team will have fun and will learn interesting and useful concepts, it is highly unlikely that the team will be any more "built" than it was before the retreat. How many times have you gone on a team building retreat, and when you get back to the office the team is more effective together for a period of approximately three months before it reverts back to its old, dysfunctional patterns? Teams are "built" only when they can consistently perform better than they were before. It is unlikely you can achieve that after one retreat.

Real team effectiveness is based on deeply rooted patterns of interaction that do not emerge simply because team members get along well or have fun together. Building teams is best accomplished by helping teams to actually identify and work through real work-based problems. This may include some skill building or discussion of new concepts, but it must always be done in the very real context of getting work done.

Associations need to take team building more seriously by making it a part of ongoing management concerns. Build team performance into management performance reviews. Provide ongoing internal and external resources to support teams in identifying and building more successful work patterns. Allow teams the space to tackle the tougher issues like conflict and accountability, rather than encouraging them to merely get along better.

If you want to bring your senior management team to a resort for a weekend and have them do trust falls with each other, more power to you. But don't pretend this is team building. It may be a nice reward for the hard work your people have put in. They will likely emerge refreshed and relaxed, and they may learn a thing or two. But keep the team building real and make it an ongoing part of the work of your association.

Discover Strengths by Asking

David Gammel

Marcus Buckingham has written extensively about how leveraging the strengths of your employees delivers dramatically better results than correcting for their weaknesses. However, the prerequisite of that power is finding a strength in your staff about which they are passionate. Here are a few questions, including a few follow-ups, that you can ask to get at that passion:

- If you could do anything you wanted here, what would you do?
- What do you want to be doing in five years?
- What would keep you here three more years?

These follow-up questions will work for any of the above to help you dig a little deeper and then tie it back to how you can leverage that passion:

- What are the steps you need to take to get there?
- Let's talk about how we can work some of those things into your job and help you to reach your goal.

The key is that you have to be earnestly interested in helping them to achieve these things and be frank when you can't. Staff will immediately sense lip service, so don't bother if you don't mean it.

Silo Busters!

Amy Smith

On page 53, fellow author Jamie Notter discusses how to break up the silo mentality in associations. I want to explore why you need to do it now.

My prediction is that technology innovations are going to eventually drive the implosion of silos within our organizations. Should it be the catalyst? No, but it probably will be. Recently I sat in two different conferences where association executives were the primary audience. One was for association publication editorial staff, the other for association educators. The same key technology themes resonated with both groups, but when asked, neither group has been talking to the other. Social media tools (blogs, wikis, podcasts, etc.) are the hot new thing for education departments, communications/PR departments, government relations, IT/web, etc. Each of these groups are looking at these tools, and in many cases acquiring them without any thought to coordinating those acquisition efforts. Soon these different departments are going to realize that they have created a nightmare integration project for IT when suddenly they all want their tools integrated with the database and/or website.

The kicker is that it is not a cost-savings issue because most of these technologies are not that expensive. Rather it is a huge integration issue. When each silo determines that they need to have their tools tracked in a database, it becomes a huge resource issue for IT/web folks.

Companies got into this same mess (but on a bigger scale) with learning management systems. Many of these organizations realized that, company-wide, they were running two or three different systems—each acquired by different divisions of the company. It wasn't until the divisions that purchased these systems wanted them integrated into the company's primary database that anyone realized there was a problem.

Take Jamie's advice. Get senior management talking and create a culture of collaboration. Do it soon. You will be hard pressed to find a dynamic, growing organization working in a silo environment. Why are you?

Performance Evaluations

Jamie Notter

Performance evaluations certainly sound better in theory than they do in practice. It makes perfect sense to monitor and evaluate the performance of employees. Those who do not perform well could be corrected or terminated, thus improving the overall performance of the system. Those who perform exceptionally well could be rewarded, providing incentives for others to increase their performance. The process, in theory, seems straightforward: sit the employee down with the supervisor, perhaps with the assistance of a written form, and identify a set of goals, objectives, standards etc. at the beginning of the year, and then meet again at the end of the year to measure results against those standards.

Yet it rarely works out that way. This "theory" of performance evaluation is unfortunately riddled with questionable assumptions and an incomplete understanding of human systems and how they work. Conventional wisdom has told us for years why we need to do what we have been doing, and it is time we start challenging this wisdom based on wisdom we have gained from our actual experiences in organizations.

Conventional wisdom: When employees know their performance will be monitored and evaluated, it will motivate them to perform better.

Experiential wisdom: Performance evaluations do not motivate people—they only scare them, and fear is never a good motivator in organizations. At the end of the day, people are afraid of getting "dinged" in their evaluation. It is psychologically uncomfortable to have a "superior" give you a bad grade, so your focus turns to things that will cause you to get a good grade (not necessarily things that will help you develop or help your organization's performance). With your attention on avoiding a reprimand, you end up actually lowering your sights to the level just above that mark.

Conventional wisdom: We need the performance evaluation system to document poor performance as legal cover to our terminations.

Experiential wisdom: Yes, you need to document poor performance, but no, you do not need to do it through the performance evaluation system. Try creating a separate system specifically for documenting poor performance and keep your performance evaluation system focused on employee development and organizational performance. Once people know that their evaluations can be held against them, trust disappears, and with trust goes open expression and communication. Without open communication, the performance evaluation system cannot work.

So take a look at what your experience in your organization is telling you, and use that to redesign the performance evaluation system. Clarify the intent of the system, and revise the structure accordingly. Allow for more frequent evaluations of performance. Allow for feedback to flow in all directions (yes, bosses, it is useful to be evaluated by your subordinates). Give people the time they need to implement the system effectively. And when you are done, use your newly acquired experiential wisdom (even if unconventional) to make the necessary modifications.

Stop Rewarding "Hard Work"

MICKIE ROPS

You ask your child to clean her room. She pokes around, gets distracted, talks to her friend on the phone, and finally, three hours later, she finishes. Does she get an extra reward because she spent double the time needed to get the job done? Ridiculous. Of course not. But, how often do you find yourself or your colleagues bragging about how many hours you/they have worked? "I stayed here until ten o'clock last night." "I've been working fifty hour weeks for over a year; I deserve a raise."

A raise? For not prioritizing, not being efficient, not delegating, not asking for help? Now, we're not suggesting that all staffers who work extra hours are poking around, distracted and inefficient! Sometimes staff put in extra time to get the job done right. But, as a general rule (and with the possible exception of non-exempt employees), staff shouldn't be rewarded simply for hours on the job or "hard work." They should be rewarded based on results or outcomes.

So, if you're the one who works those long hours, don't brag about your hard work unless you've got the outcomes to back it up. Because it's not the time on the job that matters; it's what you produce. Think about what you've accomplished and toot your horn about that instead. If you're wondering why your boss doesn't seem to be impressed with your long work hours, it's because he or she isn't! Your boss doesn't (and shouldn't) care how much you work, but he or she does care *what you accomplish*.

If you're the boss, consider the example you are setting. Do your words or actions imply that working hard is praise-worthy? Do you expect your staff to go the extra mile just like you do (and that means arriving and leaving at seven)? Do you snicker at staffers who never come in early or leave late—even though they have met or exceeded all of their deadlines and goals? It is up to you to establish a culture in which putting in time is neither desirable nor laudable, but rather, outcomes are expected and rewarded. It is also up to you to be clear about what those outcomes are and what rewards will follow.

The "Unchapter"

JEFF DE CAGNA

I attended a national association conference where there was a rather robust conversation about creating local affiliate organizations. This was my first time attending this organization's events, and thus my background in associations was not well known among the participants. I saw this as an opportunity to advance my thoughts on what we have traditionally called "chapter development." Let me share them for you here:

1. Don't start a chapter.
2. Create an "unchapter" instead.
3. Do that by thinking about everything you would do to create a chapter.
4. And then do the opposite.

I can't find a good reason why we refer to local affiliate organizations as chapters, so there is no good reason to keep doing it. Call them communities, networks, clusters or something completely different, whatever floats your boat. Just don't call them chapters, because language matters. Everyone has a mental model of what a chapter is and what it does. We need to smash those mental models, and language is one way to do that.

I see no reason why our local affiliates need to duplicate the burdensome bureaucracy and chair filling of our national organizations, so let's not do that either. No officers and no board. Let's have a small coordinating council instead that can make sure people are kept up to date about what's happening. We need to streamline administration and communication.

And, in that spirit, I see no reason why our group needs to have a formal website. Just put up a blog with all of the content the members might need. It will be much easier for volunteers to handle, not to mention much easier for the members to use and far more current in terms of sharing information.

I see no reason why these groups must have monthly in-person programs or lunches. Let each group choose its own approach. Some may want quarterly programming or only virtual programming or even no formal programming at all. I see no problem with any of those approaches so long as it works for the members. Not every group needs to fit the cookie-cutter image of the traditional chapter and nor should every group do exactly the same things. The groups should differentiate, and then coordinate, cooperate and compete with each other as necessary.

I see no reason why our groups need to follow any mandate or requirement from the national organization other than staying true to vision, mission and strategy and remaining within the boundaries of legal, ethical and financial propriety. They should do their own things and do them as well as or better than anybody else, including the national organization. Forget about the parent-child relationship. Think of it as cousins instead.

Associations need to dump the traditional model of chapter development in favor of a fundamentally new way of bringing people together at the local and regional levels. We can create new models if we're willing to let go of what we know. Experiment and learn!

Underestimating Organizational Culture

JAMIE NOTTER

It is easy to jump on the culture bandwagon. You hear it everywhere in management books and keynote speeches. Even your own intuition is telling you that organizational culture matters. If you want to succeed, you need to have (please choose from among the following platitudes): a strong culture, a healthy culture, a progressive culture, an innovative culture, a proud culture, ...the list goes on.

Culture does matter, but too many associations end their exploration of culture once they have settled on one of the platitudes above. They choose a feel-good label for their culture and then command from on-high that such a culture is the priority of the organization. This is a path to disappointment, because organizational culture does not work that way.

Organizational culture is simply a collection of tacit assumptions and patterns of behavior that provide a subtext of how things are done at your organization. It has been developing and changing constantly since the organization was founded. It develops and changes whether or not leaders pay it any attention. So if you have a problem in the organization and you want to solve it, you had better understand your culture—beyond the platitudes.

Look beyond the language in your mission and vision statements. Look beyond the posters on the walls with inspirational quotes about teamwork. Look at the physical layout of your office. Look at who eats lunch together. Ask people what it takes to get things done, and when they answer, read between the lines to get at the core assumptions underlying your culture. This will provide outstanding guidance as you try to solve problems in the office.

You will likely find that sometimes the culture itself is part of the problem you are trying to solve. You'll know this when all of your very excellent problem-solving activities strangely fail. In that case, it is the culture that is defeating you, and you'll need to work on changing your culture. This is typically more evolutionary than revolutionary (although it does depend on where your organization is in the life cycle). If the solution you are trying to implement is starkly different than your current culture, give it plenty of time to take hold. Develop a program of small steps, giving each innovation time to take hold (and establish new patterns) before introducing additional changes.

In the end, jumping on the culture bandwagon is a good idea for associations. But they must take culture more seriously and recognize that creating a positive culture will come from a collection of actions throughout the organization—actions that must be cultivated and cannot be demanded or commanded.

Blogs as a Personal Management Tool

Amy Smith

No surprise that a blogger writes about the benefits of blogging, but let us take another look at this tool and some of the great personal benefits that blogging may have for you as an association executive.

How familiar does any of this sound: we travel, we work from an office, we work from home, we are busy managing work and all that life has outside of work, we work insane hours. We spend a huge amount of time working **in** our business but much less time **on** our business.

We know that working **on** the business is where growth happens. What are you doing to help capture your pearls of wisdom, late-night thoughts, and personal great ideas?

Here are some thoughts:

Thought #1: Create a personal blog as a simple, no/low-cost way to capture your ideas.

Thought #2: Not all blogs have to be public. Create a blog using a free tool like www.blogger.com and keep it private (for now).

Thought #3: Use the blog like an online diary. Play, experiment, dream, think—just get it all out of your head and into a blog post.

Thought #4: The beauty of a blog posting is that you have the ability to edit, add to it, refine it, link to resources, etc. You can create your own categories for topics as they make sense for you.

Thought #5: When you have had a chance to think through a concept fully, and you want to share it with peers, with staff, Board members, etc., you have a great tool to control the distribution.

Thought #6: You can invite people to see just one posting or your entire blog. It is a great way to get feedback on your ideas in an electronic and flexible format.

Some of my best personal learning experiences occur by reviewing and reflecting on my personal blog. I can get access to it anytime I have an Internet connection, or I can draft a posting in Word on a flight and post it later. The great thing is that I have one place to keep all of my thoughts and ideas.

Pitch the Outcomes, Not the Technology

David Gammel

Many association staff members are interested in adding blogs to the mix of communication efforts they employ. However, just coming out and pitching a blog as a solution to anything can often raise eyebrows among staff and leaders who haven't gotten on the Cluetrain yet. You need to be a bit more subtle and start by pitching the benefits of blogging rather than blogging itself.

For example, go to your boss and say something along the lines of:

"I have found a way to easily develop new content for our website every day that is highly compelling to our younger members. In fact, it would require very little investment in software or design and could be up and running almost immediately. I would need to spend about five or six hours each week working on it. I would like to start a pilot next week to test it out."

It should be hard for anyone to respond to that with anything other than "Let's do it!" This same approach should work for any technology you wish to use, so long as you have identified the valuable outcomes it will achieve for the association (assuming it will do so!).

Managing Change

JAMIE NOTTER

When associations realize that they need to do things differently in order to get different (hopefully better) results, they too often turn to the field of change management to ensure that their staff and/or members do not ruin progress by resisting the positive change. We need to stop calling these activities change management and refer to them instead by a more accurate name: "change enforcement."

Much of the advice in change management books is focused on compelling other people to do what you want them to do. It presumes that you know better than they do, and it seeks a benevolent way to get them on board. After all, firing everyone and simply orienting your new recruits to your plan seems a bit rash.

The advice in these books is not wrong—knowledge of how fear and the comfort of routine play into behavior patterns is well documented and relevant in organizations. My problem with these books is that they tend to imply that the first time you engage people in the change is when you are enforcing it. While this may happen frequently in large organizations seeking consistency across a global enterprise, this is rarely necessary in associations with significantly smaller staffs. When you only have ten people on staff, there really isn't an excuse for not engaging them earlier on in the change process.

Tradition, however, dictates that exclusion. Tradition says issues of change are relegated to the strategic conversations, which, of course, take place only among the Board and most senior management, so we've built organizational routines that reinforce those assumptions.

The good news is, this is easy to change. Simply build new routines. Specifically, build the topic of change into your routine at a lower level. Don't leave the "what are we going to do differently" conversation to the once-every-two-years strategic planning conversation (or to the "everyone get on board" change management processes). Create space on a specific meeting agenda (at least once per quarter, but more often is better) about what is changing or needs to change in the organization.

Let staff develop the agenda and facilitate the meeting. This does not mean they are in charge—decisions about what to change can still rest at the top of the hierarchy (if that's what you want). But think about it. If you are really interested in change, it makes sense to get someone other than the person who is most invested in the way things are (the leader) to lead that discussion.

Be open to where the conversation leads you, and use these interactions as a chance to discuss major decisions about change you are going to make. And if you are not going to change (despite the staff's call for change), you can use these meetings to make your rationale crystal clear. With these conversations more the routine in organizations, we will have less need for the psychology-based coercion techniques from the "change enforcement" field.

CHANGING THE WAY WE EXECUTE

Six-Month Meeting Planning Lag

David Gammel

Traditional meeting planning processes often require that a session proposal be submitted six months before the event will actually be held. Given the speed with which our world changes today, that strikes me as an unacceptably long time in which to lock-in the majority of your event's content. Certainly, some content must be planned that far out, but is it really necessary to do so for everything?

There have been many recent developments in high-tech events, where an overall level theme is established for a meeting, but then the content to be presented is decided upon by the participants themselves, on site at the meeting. How do they get speakers, you may ask? They are the attendees themselves. This kind of conference model, called an unconference, allows the event to be as closely matched to the interests of the participants as they can.

Associations should explore adapting this model if they want to empower their meetings participants to be a critical part of the experience of their event.

Reasons Not Good Enough to Invest in Certification

Mickie Rops

I often get phone calls from association executives stating they've decided to create a certification program and want to know how I can help them to make it happen. What I say next likely really annoys them—for a few minutes anyway. I suggest they consider "un-making" that decision, at least temporarily. I know that's not an easy thing to do in the association world. After all, you've already gotten approval from two task forces, three standing committees, a five-hundred-member house of delegates, and a fifty-member board of directors. But often the decision to develop a certification program is made prematurely and if it's the wrong decision, it can be a costly one.

Following are three reasons not good enough to invest in a certification program.

To Make Revenue

Associations can generate revenue from certification programs, but it usually takes several years to turn a profit, and some never do. While making revenue can certainly be a goal and/or a measure of success of a certification program, it should *not* be the primary purpose.

To Increase Attendance at Educational Events

Trust me on this one. Developing a certification program with mandated continuing education so that individuals will have to go to your conferences to get that education is *not* a good idea. Here's a better idea: Improve your conference!

Because a Competing Association Has One, And You Can Do it Better

A little secret: Every association thinks their programs are better than those of their competitors. Maybe they are, maybe they aren't, but trying to one-up the competition is not a good reason to start a certification program, especially if theirs has a solid market share already. Of course it's possible that you can create a unique and more valuable program and be successful, but this should not be the primary reason to start a program.

Sometimes an association that initially presents these not-good-enough reasons eventually determines that certification is a wise strategic decision. Sometimes they don't. The key is to agree to step back and strategically consider what you are trying to accomplish and determine if certification is the most effective strategy for accomplishing it. Yes, this may delay progress for a few months or even longer, but it may very well save your association a costly mistake or help develop a certification program that's much stronger for it.

Four Questions About Professional Development

Amy Smith

So we have collectively ranted about organizations that offer the same conference programming year after year. It amazes me that some organizations think that the topics/issues and delivery formats popular in the late nineties still resonate in 2006. Organizations that have not changed fast enough are feeling the pressure from for-profit organizations that tend to be more nimble in their program planning and delivery. This scenario begins to raise many questions, but here are some critical questions to consider:

(1) Is the head of professional development in your organization actively participating in professional development programming him- or herself? The world of professional development and adult education is undergoing profound changes (much like IT in the 1990s). Major shifts in PD are occurring every twelve to eighteen months. How much time is the head of your organization's PD programming spending learning about these changes?

(2) Is your education committee (or its equivalent) too involved in the adult learning side of things (delivery methods for content) versus providing content direction? Practitioners in a field need to stay focused on providing content guidance while PD professionals need to focus on the best way to organize, manage and deliver that content.

(3) Does your organization have an integrated professional development strategy? Is there a working PD plan that includes **all** functional areas of the organization, including special project groups, working groups, staff development, etc.?

(4) Does your budget include enough money to adequately keep your staff up to speed? Too many association educators I know often say, "We don't have enough budget money to attend that conference." I am appalled by this notion, especially if for-profit competition is an issue for your organization. For-profit educators/trainers are attending the major education and adult learning conferences. If your staff is not there, where are they going to get a competitive advantage?

Now is the time to get serious about creating a professional development strategy that integrates the needs of your members as well as the ongoing PD needs of staff. It is time to pony up the cash to pay for these PD programs for staff, especially if your organization is competing for educational dollars.

Be Original

JEFF DE CAGNA

Associations love to copy the work of other individuals and organizations. Best practices are a big thing in our community, probably because the scarcity and constraint mindset and culture of associations leads us to conclude that best practices will be easier to implement and more cost effective over time. Unfortunately for us, there is overwhelming evidence that you cannot and will not build a truly great and successful organization simply by copying others. True success and true greatness come from daring to do what others can't do or won't try.

Personally, I loathe best practices. But I do recognize that some people like them, so I'll hold off on further critique for now. I still would like to challenge those association leaders enamored with best practices to consider the truly radical and counterintuitive notion of not duplicating what others do first. Instead, dare to be original. Rather than constantly tweaking someone else's existing solutions to your context, open yourself up to fresh, different and even plainly absurd ways of thinking. Recall the words of Albert Einstein, who said, "If at first the idea is not absurd, then there is no hope for it". Take the time to consider the unique and creative contribution you, your team and your organization can make to addressing both new and long-standing challenges in surprising ways.

Best practices stifle meaningful innovation and embrace status quo thinking (I'm sorry, I held that in as long I could). But I'm not telling you anything you don't already know. Leadership isn't about driving our associations down toward the lowest common denominator. Haven't we had enough of that? Genuine leadership values and demands authenticity, creativity and originality in the work of every contributor and from the organization as a whole. Seize the opportunity to become a true pioneer, and let the laggards copy you. Before long, they will be eating your dust!

One Login to Rule Them All

DAVID GAMMEL

How would you like it if Amazon.com required you to create a new login for each of their partners when buying a non-Amazon fulfilled product? Not much, I would guess. It is clearly user-unfriendly and would rapidly diminish their partner sales.

However, many associations require exactly that of their members for their web-based services. Features such as job boards, stores, listserves and others are often more cost effective to outsource. However, most associations will allow the vendor to require their own separate login, which doesn't match the login for the main association website.

I think the time has come where any serious vendor in the association market should support authentication from another system for their product. In fact, associations should begin to demand it.

This level of integration is relatively easy to achieve via web services. Sure, each association/system will have its quirks that may require some tweaking, but the basics are well defined.

Hostile user/login management systems immediately cripple your ability to create member value on the web. We, as an industry, shouldn't tolerate it any longer.

Publishing Only Finished Products

JAMIE NOTTER

What would happen if you took the first draft of something you were writing and actually published and distributed it? We know this feels counterintuitive. Why not wait until it has been reviewed, edited, proofed, etc.? Why risk tarnishing your image by putting something out there that is still rough around the edges?

Of course, rhetorical questions like these are precisely why we are writing this book. Those questions assume that the way we used to do it is the way we should do it today—an assumption that mistakenly discounts the speed of change in today's environment. While products have traditionally been tested, refined, and developed within the walls of an organization and then released as finished goods, the influence of the software development community is changing the way things are done. The software industry has been able to grow and be more effective by actually releasing beta versions of programs. Users recognize that these products are not finished (thus not perfect), but in exchange for the rough edges, they get to provide feedback to the designers and actually have an impact on the final product. This concept has now been extended to the book publishing field as well, particularly by Pragmatic Programmers Press.

In fact, we produced a beta print version of this book in early 2006, and from the beginning we have been posting sections of the book to the online blog. We have used the feedback from the blog and reactions to the early print release to strengthen the final product.

We were not concerned about publishing the earlier draft, because we are open to seeing the value in new ways of doing things. We know that beta publishing demonstrates our trust and faith in our customers. We know that customers that are involved in the creation of the product are more likely to evangelize it. We know that the meaning and relevance of the word "polished" are changing, and we are willing to change the way we have always done things in order to be more successful. Are you?

Crank Up Your Publishing Relevance Through Digital Downloads

DAVID GAMMEL

Selling digital downloads is becoming increasingly easy to do, yet many associations have yet to explore how it could supplement their publishing activities. Selling digital products not only saves production and shipping costs, it can also allow your association to respond more rapidly to hot issues in your field by streamlining the production process.

Creating a traditional paper book can literally take years, especially for an association that uses a heavily committee-driven process. These books are often horribly out of date once they are finally published, which lessens their value and hurts sales.

Publishing short digital works, such as a PDF, can enable your association to get content out faster so that it is still topically fresh. For example, O'Reilly Publishing has just launched a series of PDF "books" that are focused on specific topics and are very short in length. They have pared down the editing processes to be as fast as possible and use fewer resources.

Covering hot topics immediately with digital products will enable your association to be more relevant to your members' most pressing issues, concerns and opportunities.

Time to Stop Thumbing Our Noses at Curriculum-Based Certificates

MICKIE ROPS

Curriculum-based certificates have been called the "stepchild" of professional certification, the implication being that they are inferior. This perception seems to stem from their inability to meet the current certification industry standards that stipulate that certifying agencies not require training programs that are directly linked to the certification examination. Indeed, at the core of a certificate program is its comprehensive training linked to its examination.

However, discounting certificates simply because they do not meet the current third-party accreditation standards (www.noca.org/ncca/ncca.htm and http://webstore.ansi.org—search for 17024) is short-sighted. Let me clarify that I am *not* implying the standards are flawed. Rather, it is my assertion that **certificates are a distinct type of credentialing program warranting their own set of quality standards.**

Now, there are a lot of programs out there called "certificates," and often that simply means a course that provides a paper certificate after completion. Curriculum-based certificates are distinct. A quality curriculum-based certificate program typically includes these elements:

- It focuses on a specialized area within a field, not an entire field.
- Its content is identified through a job analysis.
- It includes comprehensive training on the identified content (knowledge and skills).
- It includes an assessment of identified content (knowledge and skill attainment).
- Its assessment is valid and reliable for the intended purpose, and systems are in place to monitor the performance of the assessment.

The distinctions between the more common certificates granted by associations and the curriculum-based certificate should now be clear. Here are the key differences between traditional certification and a curriculum-based model.

Certification usually covers a broad body of knowledge—often an entire field. Certificates, in contrast, usually cover a focused or specialized body of knowledge within a field. For example, there wouldn't be a "certificate in nursing," or even a "certificate in pediatric nursing," but perhaps there would be a "certificate in pediatric trauma care."

In certification, the focus is on assessing *current* knowledge and skills. In a curriculum-based model, the focus is on first *training* individuals to achieve a certain knowledge and skill base and then *assessing* their attainment of it.

Certification usually has eligibility and recertification requirements. Certificates don't, although sometimes the certificates are dated (like a diploma) to encourage (or require) participants to retake the program at specific intervals to stay current.

Certification usually awards a title and initial designation (e.g., ASAE's Certified Association Executive and CAE). Certificates award a certificate (like a diploma) so that individuals can list the attainment on resumes or other similar documents (e.g., Earned Certificate of Training in Adult Weight Management, Commission on Dietetic Registration, 2005).

So the decision whether to create a certification program or a curriculum-based certificate program should be based on the current state of the field and specialty area being investigated and the goals an organization is trying to achieve.

Consider this successful model. In 1990, the American Dietetic Association (ADA) had a strategic goal of better positioning their members in the expanding (tee hee) area of weight management. Had they been short-sighted, they could have decided to create a certification in weight management. That would have provided a form of recognition and visibility for their members. However, they recognized that training was needed to advance member skill in new treatment areas before they would be prepared to be positioned in the marketplace. They could have just created training programs, but that wouldn't have directly addressed the positioning element.

Enter curriculum-based certificates. The Commission on Dietetic Registration (CDR, the credentialing agency for the ADA) created such a program. While ADA's goal was to position members in the marketplace, CDR's primary goal for the certificate was to protect the health and welfare of the public—a compatible match and reasonable aim for the certificate program. The certificate was created in much the same way as traditional certification—with a job analysis at the core. Yet, this job analysis formed the basis of not only a test content outline, but also a comprehensive curriculum. In short, participants are trained in a specific curriculum, are tested for their attainment of it, and if successful earn the certificate. Five years into it, CDR has trained and issued thousands of certificates, and its popularity shows no signs of slowing. No one complains about the registration fee, despite it being almost twice the cost of the association's annual membership. Consistently, over 95% of participants indicate they would recommend the program to a colleague. Now, have the members been better positioned in the marketplace? Has the public been better served? No quantitative data on that yet, but all indications so far are positive.

This is a unique model in the association world, and it's one to take seriously.

Learning Experiences— Not Just Conferences

AMY SMITH

In my frank opinion, the sooner associations move away from traditional conferences, the better. A highly controversial statement, I know. Merriam-Webster defines "conference" as (1) a meeting of two or more persons for discussing matters of common concern, or (2) a usually formal interchange of views.

We would argue that many conferences do a terrible job of those two things: "discussing" and "interchange." For the first definition, we tend to subject our members to old school, classroom-style learning experiences (sometimes with dimmed lights) and dreaded PowerPoint presentations. Little "discussion" occurs in most of these sessions. When looking at the second definition, conference sessions rarely allow for a "formal interchange of views." They are simply one-way lectures with a few minutes of Q&A.

Ask any conference attendee where the value is, and you will most likely hear, "in the hallways" or "at the social functions." Why? This is the place where real-time business issues can be addressed, we can add our own context to our questions and discussions, and we can address the issues that are most pressing to us. Why do we not foster this interactivity and context setting across our association industry?

What would happen if you asked a typical conference attendee the following questions?

1. What is your number one most pressing business issue you need to address in the next six months?
2. What is that business issue costing your organization?
3. What kind of information or interactions do you need in order to address this issue?

4. What would you pay if you knew that you could get assistance addressing that issue by participating in a learning experience? (Notice I did not say conference.)

These four questions alone can generate some very interesting results. By simply asking these questions (instead of filling out worthless smile sheet evaluations), associations can begin to position themselves as the knowledge center of their industry or profession. This also transitions the fundamental role of association educators from learning managers to learning facilitators.

These four questions also allow educators to begin to reshape conference formats, features and functions. Instead of inviting speakers to be the "sage on the stage," you are inviting them to become the "guide on the side"—a learning facilitator. It expands the number of people you can then invite to facilitate, if they know they are not responsible for presenting content. It also confirms the need to create knowledge resources before, during and after face-to-face meetings.

Social networking tools (blogs, wikis, podcasts, etc.) help individuals connect in a way that was never possible before. Using these tools as a way to generate grassroots knowledge adds significant value to the learning experience. In addition, it can make face-to-face experiences more valuable, because members can network with peers electronically beforehand, get useful information just in time, and can interact with individuals and information in a way that is not currently widespread.

As you begin a new planning cycle for conferences, why not completely rethink the way you host learning experiences?

We Cannot Be All Things to All People

Jeff De Cagna

I'm pretty sure I don't need to write too much here, but in case you're wondering why, here are my three simple, one-sentence answers:

1. **It can't be done.** Can you think of any organization that does all things equally well?
2. **It shouldn't be done.** Can you think of a good reason to pursue a strategy that sets up everyone in the organization for frustration and failure?
3. **It doesn't work anyway.** Can you think of a good reason why anyone would want to be member of an association that doesn't get the first two?

Instead of being everything to everyone, consider being a single thing for most people, and let the others figure out where and how they want to play. I can't tell you what that thing is, because it is going to be different for every organization. There are no ready-made answers to be had here. Discovering what your association's one thing should be is the whole point of strategy, but we tend to overlook this basic fact while we're busy administering the thousand-and-one details contained in our multi-year, multi-page, multi-goal, multi-objective, multi-tactic and largely all-things-to-all-people strategic plans.

Why are we making it so hard, when we could be making it easier on ourselves and our members? Give up the illusion that being all things to all people is either desirable or achievable. Instead, focus on the genuine strategic opportunities that will emerge as soon as you begin looking at the world in a new way.

Content Is No Longer King

MICKIE ROPS

It's uttered in association professional development circles all the time: Content is king. But there's a new queen in town, and her name is context.

While most associations still shout out that they are the source for information in the field, the reality often is that they are a source among many others, such as competing associations, entrepreneurs— both member and non-member and maybe even past staff—and for-profits of all kinds. They are delivering content via journals, magazines, blogs, white papers, books, conferences, e-learning, among others. Take a few minutes to consider what other sources provide content related to your association's field.

It is no longer enough to provide content. Associations need to provide context too.

Consider a typical association conference. Fifty to one hundred sessions on different topics, targeted to different levels, with speakers rolling in and out for their sessions only. Some speakers are experts that can speak broadly and others are novices who speak only to their limited experiences. Attendees are on content overload—they are receiving isolated bits of information, but there is usually little to no context. And context is critical for understanding and thus for learning because it is context that gives meaning to content.

So how can you provide context? Frankly, it's easier and better done in a more intimate setting, but here are a few ideas for a more context-rich association conference:

• Change the way you organize conferences. Don't just plan lots of random individual sessions. Tracks are better, but not enough. Plan the tracks as coordinated curricula with identified learning objectives for each session that complement and build upon each other.

- Provide pre-conference recommended readings to attendees to set the stage for the material they are about to learn.
- Encourage speakers to build meaningful case studies and problem-solving activities into their sessions.
- Build lots of peer-to-peer sharing into the event, both structured and unstructured.
- Host a conference wiki with pre-established pages for each session. (You could include recommended readings here.) Encourage attendees to share their session notes, questions, and comments with other attendees on the wiki during and after the event. Encourage the presenters to read and contribute to the wiki also.
- Continue the conversations post-conference with listserve discussions or online communities.
- Consider also how you can provide context to the content on your Website, in your journals or magazines, in books, in e-learning courses or elsewhere.

Stop Storing Social Security Numbers

David Gammel

It seems that you can't go a day without reading about an organization that has had sensitive data about their customers comprised via an insecure network or stolen computer equipment. In almost all cases, these companies, government agencies and non-profit organizations had policies in place to prevent this data theft. However, the weak link, as always, was poorly trained or reckless staff who exposed the data to theft.

One thing associations can do is to stop asking for Social Security Numbers from their members. Many groups have used this ID number as a way to track applicants for certification and other programs. In the pre-Internet days, this created little risk. However in today's world the risk of this data being stolen is much higher and the potential backlash from members if you lose their data is huge.

Associations should come up with some other way of uniquely identifying their members and abandon SSNs. Purge them from your database if you already have them. The risk is too great, and earning back the trust of your members after a data incident will take too long. Protect yourselves and your members by getting rid of SSNs in your databases.

Ignoring the Means

Jamie Notter

Association executives are understandably results-focused (pardon the jargon). The CEO of an association answers to the Board—a group of people who are not expected to be experienced in running nonprofit organizations, and are expected to change positions or rotate off the board every year. If you want to keep your job in this context, then you had better produce visible results.

With this focus on results, however, comes a tendency to ignore the very powerful impact of the means used to produce those results. There are always several paths to the results we seek, and the choices we make along those paths have real consequences for staff, volunteers, and other stakeholders as well. While the attitude of "I don't care what it takes, let's just get it done" is in fact admired in our culture, it can get you into trouble.

For example, several researchers in the area of emotional intelligence in the workplace have noted that the "pacesetter" style of leadership is only effective in the short term. Leaders that drive people hard—and in the process run roughshod over emotions and relationships—may produce results in the short term, but over the long-term the negative impact of that behavior on other people in the office takes its toll. Systems cannot sustain themselves in that kind of environment, and long-term results are better supported by environments marked by understanding, compassion and empowerment.

It doesn't need to be a harsh, pace-setting environment, however, for the focus on results to become a problem. Too many associations, for example, end up putting too much pressure on their senior staff to get things done (and done right). Out of a desire to get things done, senior staff in associations often end up hoarding work to themselves. It's easier to just do it themselves, they argue, than to include other staff in the process or delegate parts of the work to others in the organization. While it is true that when they do it themselves they generate good results, they also create an environment where talented younger staff learn that they are not trusted to do substantive work. This will sap initiative from these younger workers and likely lead to higher turnover. The time saved and the decreased risk of quality problems are often offset by overall productivity and turnover costs.

Even at the Board level, the means are just as important as the ends. Too many associations hire consultants to deliver complex strategic planning processes that focus almost exclusively on the ends—an elegant and detailed strategic plan. In most cases, they are successful in generating those results (the plans are quite nice!), but in the process they have failed to develop the capacity of the Board or the staff to think or act strategically on an ongoing basis. How you develop the plan is as important (if not more important) than the plan that emerges. With increased attention to the means, you can still generate a clear strategy, but you can do it in a way that will actually increase the chances of an organization being able to leverage the strategy for long-term results.

Obviously some balance is required here; focusing too much on process can be equally debilitating, and we do see that in associations. But in the long run, knowing that *the means to an end is an end in itself* is a far more efficient and effective management principle than *the ends justify the means.*

Who Is Planning That Program?

Amy Smith

Recently I was invited to participate on the conference planning committee for a professional association to which I belong. I was very honored to be asked and willingly participated in the first (and only) conference planning call. During the call I expressed a few ideas but spent most of the time listening to the conversation. What was not made clear until the conference was that the conference chair (a Board member) had no intention of including members in the planning process. She simply went ahead and created the program.

This situation really begs an interesting question: Why bother asking members to participate on a volunteer committee, if you are not going to use their advice and input?

I think this scenario speaks to several big issues:

1. Who in your organization appoints the conference chair? Is this person the right person to lead this effort?
2. If staff plans conference content, does the staff come from the industry? If not, I would argue that volunteer input is critical.

Food for thought: Association staffers need to realize that program decision-making needs to be a collaborative process with practitioners from the field providing significant input and, more importantly, making decisions. Volunteers need to realize that association staffers know how to plan the details of events and are really good at executing events. Each party needs to stay in their own area of expertise.

Beyond Programming Education

MICKIE ROPS

Almost all associations offer learning opportunities to members. But very few do much beyond programming courses or packaging content in books. Very few actually help members become effective learners. Yet, research has shown that many of our members aren't skilled learners and that learning becomes more effective when individuals engage in several coordinated activities:

- Reflecting on current practice to establish professional direction and goals
- Identifying the gap between current and desired/needed knowledge, skills, and abilities (KSAs)
- Developing a learning plan based on identified gaps
- Selecting and participating in learning activities that address goals and targeted KSAs
- Evaluating how/if learning has been integrated into practice and what progress has been made in meeting professional goals

Associations can and should play an important role in providing support and tools in these areas to help members become more effective learners. **Programming education just isn't enough.**

Less Paper Rather than Paperless

DAVID GAMMEL

Associations are beginning to try taking their conferences paperless. No more handouts on chairs, no more frantic photocopying late into the night. All handouts are available via the conference website and/or a jump drive given to attendees. This saves the association a lot of money, and attendees don't have to damage their spinal columns adding a few pounds of paper to their luggage for the trip home.

However there is one problem. Attendees actually like to have a handout in the room to refer to. Paper still has a pretty high usability factor. Speakers also like to have the ability to put something in front of attendees, especially if it provides a useful reference for them during the session. What to do?

One solution is to print less paper rather than none. Limit speakers to a single 8.5 x 11 page, front and back, for an in-room handout. This should not be a tiny set of slides. It should be critical information the attendees should have in front of them during the session. The conference organizers can still put extended handouts online or on a jump drive for people to review in depth once they get home.

Providing one-page paper handouts allows you to continue to provide a valuable resource in the room while still gaining most of the benefits of going fully paperless. It also encourages speakers to do more than provide redundant "slideuments."

No More Checkbook Members

JEFF DE CAGNA

Am I the only one who thinks the notion of the "checkbook member," i.e., the member who writes a check once a year so he or she can receive a magazine or other materials, is a genuine tragedy?

Frankly, I find the whole phenomenon of the checkbook member—not to mention the matter-of-fact way so many association professionals speak of it—to be a bit of an embarrassment for our community. In a time when tens of thousands of software developers are volunteering to create open source applications and so many of our organizations are struggling to find qualified contributors to our work, I think it is extraordinarily unfortunate that we call someone a member simply because he pays dues each year.

From my perspective, a member is someone who contributes to the organization's work in some tangible or intangible way beyond the initial financial transaction. It doesn't have to be a big and time-consuming contribution, but it must involve something that creates value directly for other members, the organization or the field as a whole. After all, our organizations are not credit card companies, and membership in them should not be defined by the act of making payment. Associations are about authentic relationships. And such relationships can form only between people who are interested in creating and sustaining them over time. If membership affords us certain privileges, it also requires that we accept certain responsibilities.

So, let's do a little math. Let's say my organization has 20,000 members, of which perhaps 10% are actually contributing in some manner to association activities. To my way of thinking, I actually have a membership of 2,000 and a subscriber base of 18,000 people. Why should I include in a membership count people who demonstrate no interest in making a meaningful contribution to the organization's success? To enhance my clout in public policy? To satisfy my board's desire to see the raw membership numbers increase every year? To burnish my own resume? We may use these rationalizations to explain our thinking, but that doesn't make us right.

From a business model perspective, the end of the checkbook member would be a real plus for most associations. If they would reclassify their checkbook members as subscribers, I believe many organizations would dramatically increase their revenues very quickly. Freed from having to underprice valuable offers in the name of good member service, associations could charge subscribers whatever the market would bear. In fact, I think getting rid of the checkbook member would actually be a very positive development for the soul of the association membership function. Once the difference between members and customers (or members and subscribers) is absolutely crystal clear, it will challenge all of us to figure out what we really value and exactly how much we value it. That can only be a good thing.

Will Traditional Certification Meet Future Needs?

MICKIE ROPS

For many fields, it may be time to rethink the traditional model of professional certification in order to meet the needs of the changing workplace environment and workers.

Say I'm considering changing careers and am interested in your profession. I google the field and click to your website to investigate what I need to do. First, I discover I need a bachelor's degree. Alright, I've got that. Oh, wait, it needs to be in x or y. Mine's in z. Strike one. And it needs to be from a university accredited by your association. Although mine is a regionally accredited college, it's not on your short list. Strike two. Oh, I need seven years of experience before I can get the credential anyway. That seems like forever. Strike three. I decide to check out the online Occupational Outlook Handbook (www.bls.gov/oco) and discover the crazy part—the certification is voluntary. All this and I don't even need it? Plus, there's no state regulation of the industry.

Back to Google. What's this? A university certificate program offered online...a corporate certification program...another association's intensive training program...lots of appealing options that fit my needs.

You're thinking, okay, so we have eligibility requirements, but they are all necessary to ensure the quality and meaning of the credential. That will be true for some professions, but definitely not all. Consider if yours are *really* necessary or if there can be alternate pathways. Is an academic degree necessary or can some combination of training and work experience substitute? Does the academic degree have to be discipline-specific or can additional training substitute? Do you have any requirements that serve as artificial barriers to earning certification? Is there really any evidence an individual not meeting the requirements is any less qualified than those that do?

Now, consider the projection that Millennials (sometimes called Generation Y or Generation Next—those currently entering the workplace) will engage in an average of six careers in their professional life. Yes, that's careers, not jobs. Now in that light, consider again the traditional model of certification. How many Millennials are going to be willing to go to a college you deem acceptable to get a degree you deem acceptable just to get a credential that is voluntary? What about those who already have a base degree and are in the workforce? **Does your certification have enough value in the market to drive an individual to basically start over? Are you confident you can sustain that value positioning for the next ten years? Or twenty?**

I'm not suggesting that standards be watered down. But at minimum, credentialing bodies need to take a hard look at what artificial barriers they can remove. And in some cases, the whole certification model may need to change.

The half-life of knowledge in many fields is decreasing rapidly, and fields are becoming more specialized. It may well be the current model of certification just won't work for your field anymore. As one possibility, just-in-time credentialing may be a more viable model in the new marketplace.

Consider the just-in-time model occurring in parts of the IT industry. A new technology solution emerges so you get real life work experience. Take a comprehensive training program, if you need it. Take a performance-based test to prove your competence. Earn a certification. Gain a new skill set and a resume-enhancer to position yourself better in the job market. A new technology solution emerges and the cycle begins again…and again…and again.

This model has already proven successful in the IT industry. Maybe there's something to be learned here for your field. Or maybe an entirely new model needs to emerge. **One thing is certain: you cannot assume that the traditional model of certification is going to meet future needs. It may not already.**

.Org Sites Shouldn't Be Org Charts

DAVID GAMMEL

Even today, too many associations drive their website design and structure by how they work internally. This usually comes from simply extending current operations to the Web, rather than thinking about the entirety of their website and how well it serves their mission and members. Not having a single person who is ultimately responsible for the overall direction and success of the site contributes to this problem as well.

Associations must consider their websites from the perspective of their members and other site visitors. Why do members come to your site? What do they want to accomplish? How can your website provide value to them? Answering those questions will put you on the path to creating a site that meets their needs.

Just Do It—Now!

AMY SMITH

What would happen if you gathered fifteen to twenty of the brightest, up-and-coming members you have and asked them to design the ideal [fill in the blank]? It could be the ideal publication, product, learning event, interaction, membership structure, etc.

What would happen if you added some non-industry bright minds to that mix?

And what would happen if you kept the staff and known leaders of the organization out of that conversation?

How quickly could your association organize this gathering? Hours, days, weeks, months, years?

How quickly could you act on the group's ideas? Hours, days, weeks, months, years?

What political hoops would the group or staff have to go through in order to execute the idea?

The biggest questions of all: How can you create an environment that is free of the political oversight of the organization and gets executed in the most expeditious manner possible?

Think of the great things that could come from this!

Radical Simplicity

Jeff De Cagna

"Simplicity is the ultimate sophistication."
(Leonardo da Vinci)

We need to make our organizations easier, clearer and simpler for everyone involved. We need to consistently, carefully and firmly identify everything we do that isn't fundamental to advancing our larger purposes and do away with those things as quickly as possible. This is what I mean by "radical simplicity." In today's world, less is not only more, **much less is much more.**

In recent months, I have come to view radical simplicity as a major strategic opportunity for associations that touches all aspects of what we do, from governance to products and services to volunteer engagement. In far too many organizations in our community, the complexity we create ourselves interferes with our ability to achieve what we say we care about most, including supporting learning, building vibrant communities and delivering value to those we serve. We live in a complicated world to be sure, and there isn't much we can do to change that, except to the extent we are able to change how our organizations relate to it.

> *"As simple as possible, but no simpler."*
> *(Albert Einstein)*

By suggesting we make radical simplicity a priority, I do not mean to suggest we should dumb down our organizations. On the contrary, our associations should be the hottest of hothouses, in which we plant the seeds of many new innovations, nurture them and allow them to grow in all kinds of intriguing and unexpected directions. There is an important difference between the organic evolution of complexity in our thinking and the creation of synthetic complexity that so often occurs in our organizations. The former is a natural cycle of growth and change that systematically builds our capacity. The latter involves the unnatural and unnecessary introduction of hierarchical and bureaucratic constraints into places and spaces where, if we took the initiative to cultivate them, trust, reciprocity and the capacity for self-organization would serve us very well.

Radical simplicity isn't about avoiding complexity altogether. It is about creating a markedly more intuitive and straightforward interface between our organizations and our members that enables all of us to make better sense of the complexity we need and drastically reduces (if not eliminates altogether) the complexity we don't.

> *"What is the simplest thing that could possibly work?"*
> *(Ward Cunningham, inventor of the wiki.)*

On a very practical level, embracing radical simplicity in our work might make the difference between robust growth and anemic performance in key metrics. At a minimum, a radically simpler organization should make for happier and more satisfied staff and members. For me, a focus on radical simplicity is itself a form of genuine innovation, and one that definitely can make a meaningful impact along multiple dimensions quickly.

To set your organization down the path of radical simplicity, consider raising the following five questions for discussion:

- What factors create complexity in your association's work?
- How much of the complexity in your association is self-inflicted?
- How do tried-and-true solutions actually increase complexity in your organization?
- Why does your association have difficulty letting go of just about anything?
- What are the elements of a new business model that will allow your association to fully embrace radical simplicity?

To put your strategic thinking into action, consider one final inquiry: **What three things about your association can you radically simplify in the next three months?** If you can initiate these critical conversations, you will go a long way toward creating the right conditions for enduring success in your association.

Forget Your Navigation for a Day

David Gammel

Association staff and leadership website discussions often focus on their navigation. Website navigation is hierarchical by nature and hierarchies imply relative values between the listed items. Top billing in the navigation system will usually be interpreted as an indicator of importance by content stake holders, which then leads to inevitable tugs-of-war over placement and wording.

My suggestion for the next time that conversation comes up: forget about navigation. What if your site had no navigation? What other tools do you have at your disposal to guide traffic around your site? (Hint: search and the content of your main entry pages!) How can those be used to effectively highlight the content and services you want to get in front of your members?

Having a conversation without navigation will allow you to use the totality of your site much more effectively.

CHANGING THE WAY WE WORK TOGETHER

Fearing Conflict

JAMIE NOTTER

Why is everyone afraid of conflict? The board, members, committees, staff groups, leaders, followers—the one thing they all have in common is that they are afraid to confront each other with conflicts or significant differences in opinions.

For example, an association executive recently asked advice from colleagues on a listserve about what to do about a committee co-chair who had "done a lot of work...but stepped on lots of toes and caused extra work for staff." The incoming president was suggesting not reappointing this person as co-chair.

Instead of dealing with the conflict, the first response is to end the relationship. Unfortunately, this response is typical. At all levels of associations, people bury conflict. They hide it. They ignore it. They pretend it isn't conflict. They lie about it. If it gets really bad, they raise the stakes and take actions that simply remove the possibility of the conflict emerging again (e.g., ending the relationship). People will do anything but confronting it head on (like, for example, having a candid conversation with a volunteer about how his behavior is upsetting other volunteers or staff).

Of course, there is a valid explanation for chronic conflict avoidance. Everyone has had experiences of being in conflict where the situation got uncomfortable, tense, maybe even painful and frustrating. That's why we run the other way. But remember, just because conflict has been unpleasant, doesn't mean it always will be. Conflict is a natural part of every single human system, so instead of trying to avoid it (which is impossible), how about learning how to deal with it more effectively?

The good news is, it isn't rocket science. It takes a little bit of knowledge and perhaps some skill development, but mostly it takes the courage to simply try a new approach. Start small on the less important conflicts, and as you make progress you can tackle the bigger issues. But above all, start. The cost of ignoring conflict can be overwhelming.

When conflict is avoided, the real issues never get out on the table. A pattern will then emerge in your association where the norm is to hide what you really think (or at best vent about it at the water cooler). So at meetings, people talk around the difficult issues, retiring to their offices without a clear sense of what agreements were made or what they should do next. In fact, in cultures where conflict is routinely avoided, being accountable becomes quite difficult, and results suffer—all because we were afraid to deal with conflict.

So it may feel like it would be less painful to avoid that conflict, but don't be fooled. In the long run you will suffer more by avoiding it. Start paying attention to the conflict in your association. Notice where it happens and notice when you and others avoid it. Then start the work of changing the pattern and dealing with your conflict differently. The long-term payoff can be significant.

Diversity as a Numbers Game

MICKIE ROPS

Diversity is given a lot of lip service in associations. We see diversity initiatives, diversity committees, diversity scholarships, and more. However, diversity is most often viewed as a necessary evil at worst and a numbers game at best. Members of diverse groups (of a different nationality, gender, age, etc., than the average member) are purposefully placed on boards and committees to meet diversity goals and/or to be politically correct.

Diversity is usually not seen for what it really is: a business strategy. As Frans Johansson, author of *The Medici Effect*, has recently expressed so well, diversity brings greater potential for a wider range of perspectives and ideas, which can lead to new and improved products and services. A great strategy for getting out of the "we've always done it that way" mentality would be to truly embrace diversity and the value it could bring to your association.

And, contrary to popular belief, probably the first clue that an association hasn't fully embraced diversity is that it still has a diversity committee.

The Power of Transparency

JEFF DE CAGNA

I recently met a former flight attendant who knows a great deal about my preferred carrier, United Airlines. (She did not work for United, but for one of its partners.) As a United frequent flyer, I was interested to hear the story behind the airline's decision to offer Channel 9, the on-board audio channel that gives passengers the opportunity to listen to communications between the cockpit and air traffic control. As an anxious air traveler, I rely on Channel 9 as a tool for relaxing during my flights. I frequently tell others that listening to the cockpit, while it might sound quite boring, is actually quite interesting because the exchanges between the pilots and ATC are always so polite and professional, and reflect genuine competence. It is such a refreshing change of pace from so many workplace conversations, which often are laden with hidden meanings and political agendas, and sometimes try to mask incompetence. In contrast, when a pilot is told by an air traffic controller to "descend and maintain 1-5-0," or 15,000 feet, the response is always, "1-5-0, United 540" or whatever the specific flight number might be. No arguments, no politics, no BS.

But things apparently were quite different before the introduction of Channel 9. In the aftermath of President Reagan's firing of air traffic controllers in 1981, there was significant vitriol between pilots and air traffic controllers at United. From what my acquaintance told me, I gather that yelling and cursing were commonplace in communications between planes and ATC. In fact, by the late 1990s, when Washington, D.C.'s National Airport was renamed for President Reagan, pilots calling ATC using "Reagan" would simply be ignored by the tower, creating a remarkably unsafe situation.

United management tried many approaches to ameliorate these problems without success. Finally, there was a brainstorm, and a decision was made: **All ATC-cockpit conversations would be made available to passengers!** The airline secured the necessary approvals and the whole game changed. Now, the air traffic controllers and pilots had to clean up their act or face the wrath of the flying public. Obviously, they chose the former, because if they hadn't, United certainly would not exist today (not that it's out of the woods by any means).

This story compels me to ask association leaders a question: **What would your members hear in your HQ office or boardroom if they could listen in to their own association-specific Channel 9?** Would they admire the professionalism and competence of your staff or board, or would they simply wonder what the heck is going on? Transparency clearly has been a very powerful tool for shifting both thinking and action at United, and it can be for your association as well.

Emotional Ignorance

Jamie Notter

In popularizing the concept of emotional intelligence, Daniel Goleman and other researchers have challenged our traditional definition of "smart" (people who did well in school and scored well on tests like the IQ test that measured our reason, logic, memorization, and analytical capacity). According to their research, measures of "emotional intelligence" (being able to manage and express feelings, having empathy for others, understanding and managing social relationships, etc.) are a better predictor of success than traditional measures of intelligence. Goleman links emotional intelligence with effective leadership as well.

So why aren't associations listening? We may invite Goleman to speak at our conferences, but typically we ignore much of what he says in the way we run our associations, at both the staff and volunteer levels. For example, expression of emotions is typically all but outlawed in staff interactions. It is often considered unprofessional to express emotions in the workplace, and people who express emotions regularly are often labeled as "problem" people on the staff. This is, itself, a problem. While there is certainly room for limits (no one wants temper tantrums during the staff meeting), it is actually counterproductive to completely suppress emotions.

The primary reason is that we all have our emotions whether we want to or not. The emotional center of your brain sends its electric signals out much faster than the rational center, which means you will have your emotional reaction even before you have a chance to rationalize it away. Inability to express emotions can create pressure that builds up over time, which ends up getting in the way of work performance, or even in the very intense emotional expression that you were trying to avoid in the first place.

Yet there are ways to accept emotions as a part of the workplace and still uphold standards of professionalism. Supporting people in accepting simple emotional expression as permissible in the workplace can actually facilitate people's ability to deal with issues as they arise. The suppression of emotion supports the nasty habit of avoiding all conflict, so removing that barrier actually supports a more direct and productive environment.

In addition to expression, of course, you can also support performance by more effectively managing emotions internally. Expressions of emotion are usually greatly outnumbered by the number of times our emotional "buttons" get pushed in the office, triggering an internal emotional reaction that tends to get in the way with us successfully doing our work. Simply being aware of this and developing techniques for managing this internally can also support a more productive and professional expression of emotion.

It is simple and effective. It does not make the workplace "touchy-feely," and there is very little danger of spontaneous singing of "Kumbaya." With just a little more tolerance and support of emotions, you will simply get more done.

Recruiting Gen X Women

Amy Smith

The Always Done It That Way crew is made up of five Gen Xers (in case you have not figured that out by now). This does not mean we have all the answers about Generation X, but we do have some insight.

Very recently I attended a professional association conference (of which I am a member), where the membership is all women. I belong to a few of these groups, so identification will be difficult (although several of these groups are dealing with the same issue). They want to recruit young Gen X and Millennial women to join the organization and to eventually be on the Board. Many associations are discussing the issue of how to recruit younger members. I cannot speak for my entire generation, but I do have some insight on recruiting Gen X women.

Background

The Board of this organization is mostly women fifty-five and older, with a couple of token forty-somethings. It is basically the female version of the old white male Board structure we see in the association world. The Board selected a keynoter—an over-fifty-five white female—for the conference who spoke about generational issues using data that was at least ten years out of date. The requirements to sit on the Board include attendance at the two annual conferences the organization hosts, plus a whole bunch of other hoops. From an educational point of view, the content at the conference is weak, thus few people beyond senior volunteer leaders attend. Sessions are led, again, by Baby Boomer women, and this time a few minority women are included in the bunch.

Are you seeing the picture yet?

The one saving grace: the Board did have enough sense to hire a GenX female Executive Director (she's fabulous!). Unfortunately, I am not sure how much guidance they really take from her. But I do have to give the Board credit for recognizing that they need to make significant changes to the organization to exist going forward.

After the first day of the conference I cannot tell you how many Board members pulled me and the few other GenX participants aside to ask how the organization can do a better job of recruiting members "like us."

Here is my off-the-top-of-my-head snapshot of what your association is competing with right now. And keep in mind, GenX women are dealing with many of the same issues.

GenX women are of child bearing age. I happen to have:

- two small children (aged one and three).
- a husband who likes to see my face occasionally versus our long daily string of instant messages.
- a growing business (and travel quite a bit); the office manager often questions who I am.
- a large family and a group of friends, all of whom wonder where I am most of the time.
- a stack of fifty great business books and industry publications sitting in my office that I want to get to.
- a laundry list of business questions I want answers to now, not in six months when the next conference takes place.

Frankly, many of these issues are not GenX specific. However, I would add the following general characteristics.

First, my generation of women is the first to fully view ourselves as peers and equals to our male counterparts. Title IX helped with that. We outperformed our male counterparts in college, and we are the first generation to graduate in larger numbers than men. We have the expectation that we will be treated equally in the workplace, and we do not tolerate the males being paid more for the same work. We expect equality with men *and* women—and, frankly, everyone.

Second, we watched our loyal Baby Boomer parents get fired and laid off from companies they spent their whole lives serving. So we are not too interested in organizational loyalty. You will have to prove it to us that participation in your association is truly valuable to our professional goals.

On top of these generational issues, I also have two big business issues pressing for me now: (1) how to create a business "dashboard" that includes financial and other data that relates to a growing consulting practice, and (2) I want to meet three to five other business consultants who have growing consulting practices. I want to get in a room with them for a day and pick their brains. However, this format is not available at the conference. It is just a whole bunch of speakers spreading their "wisdom" about business issues. Because most organizations are not meeting my needs, I'm happy to go out and create one that does. (Except for this one little quirk, I personally, happen to know the value of association participation, so you won't see me doing that anytime soon.)

So to sit on the Board or become a more senior leader within the organization you are asking us GenX women to spend $500+ on registration, $200+tax a night on hotel for three nights, plus travel to attend a two-day conference with questionable content? All so I can sit on the Board to represent the GenX crowd and possibly help you fix your recruitment problem?

Here is my free advice on your recruitment problem:

(1) Ask GenXers what it takes to get them to join a professional association. Do not listen to consultants or anyone else—especially those with out-of-date generational information.

(2) *Listen, listen, listen!* Actually listen to what GenXers have to say.

(3) Do something about it today—not create a two-year plan on recruiting GenXers. Make the changes quickly. If you struggle to do this, just empower some GenXers to do it. They will get it done, and well.

(4) Get smart GenX members into the organization at the highest levels, and not just one token GenXer at the Board table. If that means you have to loosen some of your requirements, do so.

(5) Make membership valuable. Provide challenging and interesting content presented by a wide range of people and allow for opportunities to collaborate with other like-minded members.

If your organization takes too long to make significant changes to attract GenXers, they will go start a competing organization that meets their needs. In this day and age it is easy to do.

Most Memos to All Shouldn't Be

DAVID GAMMEL

One thing that any organization should curtail are memos to all staff that are in response to one person violating a policy or procedure.

I am sure you have recently encountered, if not authored, one of these beastly things. Bashing all staff about the dress code, length of lunch break, or other policy violation when the issue is in response to the acts of a single person is cowardice, plain and simple. Have frank conversations with staff members who are out of line. If you can't bring yourself to speak with them individually and provide appropriate feedback, at least avoid the temptation to memo the whole staff.

These types of memos to all hurt employee morale and are usually quite transparent to staff as to who they are really about. Either have the courage to actually manage your individual staff or the wisdom to not slam your entire office over an individual's problems.

Attitude Trumps All

MICKIE ROPS

How many times have you kept a position open while looking for that someone with the perfect credentials, experience and/or expertise for your association job? I think experience and expertise are overrated. Even this certification consultant has to admit that credentials are trumped too. Let's face it; there are many jobs within an association for which attitude is *way* more important.

Dealing with members all day can be challenging. I used to work for a certifying agency, and during certain periods I took call after call from individuals who had failed a certification exam (including a few members of the Board of Directors). It takes a person with a special attitudinal gift to handle calls like those with grace (and frankly, that person likely isn't me).

I understand the desire to hire staff with association experience, since association work is often quite different from the corporate world. But honestly, have you *ever* hired a genuinely nice person that wasn't able to "get" the member focus? And, given how easy it was for these authors to come up with 101 things about associations that must change, perhaps an outside view wouldn't hurt!

In many association jobs, experience, credentials, etc. mean little if your staff member has a lousy attitude. I'm confident you can train a person how to do many association jobs, but can you teach a rude person to be pleasant? A slug to be energetic? Someone who's apathetic to be driven?

Next time you're hiring, look for experience, expertise, credentials, *and* attitude, but don't settle for the former three without the latter.

CEO Gender Pay Equity

Amy Smith

The June 6th issue of *Associations Now* offers an interesting glimpse into salary equity (or inequity) for association staff. The article, "Determining Your Present Value" is a summary of the recently published *Association Executive Compensation & Benefits Study, 1st Edition*, published earlier this year by ASAE & The Center for Association Leadership. While most of the statistics do not seem to surprise me at all, Figure 3 seems to really annoy me. This is the CEO Median Total Compensation by gender. It compares total compensation by staff size and gender and provides comparative information based on the 2004 study.

The figure shows that for an association with an average staff size of 21–50, male CEOs make an average of $243,000 annually compared to $181,000 for their female counterparts. This may not be so surprising to you, but what is appalling is that in the 2004 study, the report indicates male and female salaries of $231,000 and $173,000 respectively. The 2004 difference is $58,000. You would expect that the gap is closing, but based on this article, it is, in fact, widening. The 2006 gap is $62,000.

So why in the world is this happening? One might suggest that male CEOs report more experience, but in fact, in this study both males and females reported a median of six years experience in the position.

I think this article begs several questions, but here is a kicker: What up-and-coming female executive wants to run an organization and get paid less than her male counterparts? If she is coming from GenX or the Millennials, the quick answer is, no one.

Our generations view our male counterparts as equals—no better than we are. We fully expect gender pay equity. What will happen to those GenX and Millennial women who aspire to be association CEOs one day, who view this study and rethink their professional choice? Maybe they will jump to the "dark side" and become consultants as many of us have.

Focusing on the "Problem" Person

JAMIE NOTTER

"Everything would be fine if it weren't for [fill in the blank]."

How often have you heard such a statement in an association? This person could be a rank-and-file member, someone on the Board, or a staff person at any level. Whoever it is, he or she definitely a problem, or too often, the problem.

As such, the solutions associations develop in response tend to be focused on that individual "problem person." But this too often makes matters worse. While it is true that there are individuals whose behavior or attitude can negatively impact the performance of an organization, it is rarely a case of simple cause and effect. Organizations are complex systems. Looking only at the problem person leaves out too many other important factors, so solutions that focus on the problem person usually fall short. As quality guru W. Edwards Deming said, "defects are always a sign of system failure."

Consider three typical responses to problem people.

Termination

The obvious solution to a problem is to get rid of it. For staff, this means termination. If they are volunteers, it's a bit trickier, but let's be honest—there are ways to leverage the volunteer system to ensure that certain people do not volunteer any more. While in some cases, termination takes care of the problem behavior, in too many cases it does not. The problem behavior pops up in the form of a new individual. Problem people are often reflecting a frustration in the system. While it seems like it is one person's personality (and that certainly would play a role), as long as the root frustration in the system is not addressed, new problem people are bound to emerge.

Write a policy

If you are afraid to get rid of the problem person, then the next means of control to which you can turn is policy. If you don't like someone's behavior, write (or enforce) a policy that outlaws that behavior. A common example of this is when one or two staff people are perceived to be abusing flex time or not putting in enough hours, and suddenly the entire staff is then forced to punch in using a time clock. While that policy may convince your problem person to put in more hours, it also generates many new problems from the people who now feel like they are not trusted or have to waste time on bureaucratic details instead of getting their work done.

Train everyone

Similar to the policy solution, providing training to everyone in the areas where the problem person is perceived to be deficient is also a common solution. If people have trouble communicating with the problem person, provide the Board with communication skills training. While this solution probably won't hurt (who couldn't use a brush up on communication skills?), it rarely solves the problem. The problem person usually sees through the ploy and gets defensive about the whole training, and the others often see it as a waste of time ("I already know how to communicate—the problem is him!"). The real value of the communication training is often lost.

So what's the solution? First of all, the solution is not simple. These three typical solutions oversimplify the situation. There is nothing wrong with firing people, writing and enforcing policies, or providing training, but do not fall into the trap of using blunt instruments like these to solve complex and delicate problems. Second, problems require direct attention, and all three of these solutions involve avoidance. Even the seemingly direct answer of termination implies a long period of avoiding the problem person as the behaviors were developing. Confronting and dealing directly with both the problems (and the problem people) on a continuous basis will often resolve the problems before they escalate.

Letting Problems Solve Us

JEFF DE CAGNA

When confronted with a problem, human beings instinctively want to solve it. Most of the time, this reflex serves us well, especially when it comes to both routine difficulties and matters of life and death. But more often than we might suspect, we are confronted with situations when it would make more sense not to follow our instincts and, instead, let the problems we face "solve us."

Solve us you ask? It is an insight that I took away from my graduate work with Professor Robert Kegan in the late 1990s. As Professor Kegan says, "We all do the best we can to cope within the world of our assumptive design." To put it another way, the assumptions we make every day about every aspect of our life experience shape the way we make sense of and interact with the world. In effect, our assumptions allow us to design the world in which we want to live, one that is often at odds with the realities others experience. We cope by trying to resolve this dissonance, which is why we are very intent on solving problems.

But what if we had sufficient awareness to recognize that our *apparent* problems might not be the *actual* problem? What if we could see that sometimes the problem is simply an indicator of flawed or, at least, untested assumptions? What if we could step outside of the problem and look at our relationship to it so that we might understand it in a new way? Without a doubt, it is easier for us to ask these questions than it is to do what they ask of us. Nevertheless, I believe what I am writing about here is an absolutely critical capability that both staff and volunteer association leaders must develop going forward.

Let's think briefly about how letting problems solve us might influence our work on strategy. Strategic planning is a clear-cut method for solving the problems we have with ambiguity, complexity and uncertainty. In strategic planning, we identify mostly what we know we know today, and we do a little bit of elaboration on it to give it a future feel. Then we pre-determine the outcomes we want to achieve and work fastidiously toward reaching them. No mess, no fuss. This approach may be clean and neat, but it is neither authentic nor pragmatic, given what we know is true about the current strategic landscape.

In contrast, letting the problem solve us challenges our assumptions along multiple dimensions, especially our commitment to wanting all the answers even before the questions are asked. Letting the problem solve us instead puts the focus on learning as we go, exercising judgment and constantly testing our assumptions. From this process, not only will we achieve different results, but our approach to strategic leadership also will be different.

So, the next time you confront a problem in your work, consider stepping back from trying to solve it immediately. Instead, see if the problem can solve you.

Stop Complaining that the Board Doesn't Get It

Mickie Rops

Over the years we've heard a lot of association executives complain about the decisions their boards or committees have made or are heading toward. "Why would they do that?" and "Man, they just don't get it," we've heard over and over again. The commonly held belief that the volunteer leaders make the decisions and staff members implement them seems to have become an easy escape from responsibility.

It's time for change. It's time to stop complaining and do something about it.

As the executive director or senior staff executive, take responsibility for informing the leadership. Make sure they have considered all the options and potential ramifications of each. Develop white papers or bring in experts. If you have a concern with the direction in which they are heading, speak up. If personal agendas are taking over, call them on it.

Of course, be smart about it—your timing and presentation are critical. And if you feel your board doesn't want or respect your opinion, then you need to consider why that is. Are you being condescending? Defensive? Seemingly biased? It's crucial that you make yourself a respected and valued part of the decision-making. Just because you may not have an official vote in the final decision doesn't mean you should just let the discussions and decisions go where they may.

Don't be a victim. Take control. Take responsibility. Will this guarantee you'll agree with all the decisions that are made? Of course not, but at least you'll know they were informed decisions.

Panic Around Generational Differences

JAMIE NOTTER

Generational differences receive a lot of attention these days, particularly in the association community, but too often the attention they get is laced with a certain amount of panic:

- All the baby boomers are retiring!
- Generation X are not "joiners!"
- Millennials only want to play video games!

As researchers begin to identify trends in values, attitudes and behavior that vary from generation to generation, association executives struggle with how to apply that information to the actual running of their business. At an association conference, a Baby Boomer executive actually suggested that the best strategy to deal with generation X is to simply wait them out. Millennials, he suggested, are joiners, so we just need to wait for them to take over the leadership positions in the association!

The panic is not helping. We need a different approach to this issue. The first step in dealing with generational shifts is to look beyond the stereotypes that have been generated over the last few years. Some of them are quite accurate, but some of them do not tell the whole story. For example, you may have noticed that there are fewer Generation X members entering your volunteer "pipeline." While they may have different attitudes about "joining" and volunteering than their predecessors, the Baby Boomers, the fact is this drop in numbers is to be expected. Generation X was the baby "bust" after the boom. The Department of Labor predicts a net decline in the middle management workforce in this country by 10% between 2000 and 2010.

Sometimes, of course, the stereotypes are accurate. Yes, generations are different. Knowledge of those differences, however, can only help you manage your association more effectively if it is paired with a critical organizational discipline that is too often neglected: the discipline of conversation. How do you manage the ongoing conversation with your members to uncover the relevance of generational differences? You know that there are generational differences, but it is only through a careful and respectful conversation with your membership that you will uncover the relevance. If younger members aren't volunteering as much, don't rely on an article to tell you why—ask them yourself. All that background information you got on Generation X will help guide the conversation, but the conclusions about what to do differently will only emerge from the conversation itself.

So the second step is to build the capacity in your association for more effective conversations. This will cut across the organization, from conversations about strategy to weekly staff meetings. As you make these conversations more effective, then apply that increased capacity to the issue of generations. Try intentionally starting some new conversations across different generations, and see where it leads. Include younger staff or members in your strategy conversations. Convene cross-generational groups to discuss a marketing campaign. Remember, the goal is not to find the static answers; the goal is to find dynamic strategies for ongoing generational renewal.

Dysfunction Cannot Be Fixed with Reorganization

Amy Smith

For the past eight years I have had an "interesting" time observing my husband's workplace—a news organization. The organization has been a part of the Gallup organization's Q12 study (see www.marcusbuckingham.com) and has undergone three significant reorganizations in eight years. Let's just say that the organization's leadership is wrought with individuals who are weak managers, but the reorgs continue.

So what can we learn from this brief profile? A few key lessons.

(1) Just because you are part of, volunteer for or pay for a management analysis of your organization does not mean that you have good managers.
(2) If you are going to subject your employees to an organizational analysis, you'd better be ready to make changes, because these studies often uncover the good, bad and ugly.
(3) If you are leading an organization through an analysis and the reporting mechanisms uncover issues to your staff, and you choose not to make significant changes in weak areas, you are putting yourself at a huge disadvantage to your employees.
(4) Not all people make good managers. Just because someone has been around a while in a functional area and done well there does not mean that they will make a good manager.
(5) Reorganizations do not fix dysfunction. If you have bad managers, they are not going to get better by being moved to other divisions. They are just going to make more employees unhappy.
(6) Find valuable work for those with tenure, but do not assume they want to be or have the ability to be a good manager.

Expecting Something Different from More of the Same

MICKIE ROPS

Frans Johansson, author of *The Medici Effect* (www.themedicieffect.com), advocates that great ideas are generated at the intersection of different fields, cultures and perspectives. Yet, how often do we expect great things from our perpetual homogeneity?

As a case in point, my husband's engineering consulting firm recently had a meeting to generate new business models for revenue generation. Guess who attended the meeting? A bunch of engineers who've worked at the firm ten or more years. Oh, and they were all forty-year-old plus white men. How many barrier-busting ideas do you think were generated there?

It's easy to chuckle at the absurdity of that, yet consider the last group of staff or volunteers you brought together. How diverse was it? And by diverse, I don't mean that you have one token minority.

It's tempting to surround ourselves with others just like us. It's natural. It's comfortable. But what's the likelihood that it's going to generate anything extraordinary? Or is it more likely they'll all sit around agreeing with each other and the status quo?

How often do we purposefully hire staff or recruit volunteers of different backgrounds? Different cultures? Different ages? Different personalities or styles? Yes, heads may knock a bit, but out of that collision may just come a few (or many) great ideas.

And when those new volunteers or staff members start to question the status quo, resist the temptation to roll your eyes with frustration that they just don't understand "how things work around here." They don't, and that's a good thing. They haven't yet been struck with the "we've always done it that way" virus. Shield them from infection, and their new perspectives may just transform your association *if* you let them.

Fighting via E-mail

Jamie Notter

E-mail is a wonderful tool, particularly for associations who need to manage communication with members and volunteers who are often spread out across the country, or even the world. Even among staff in the same building, it enables a higher volume and higher speed of communication.

Like any tool, however, e-mail is not right for every job. Take, for example, that time when you were angry with a colleague or had a conflict with a volunteer about how to manage a project. You got an e-mail from this person that you feel went one step too far. You then sat down at your computer and shot off an e-mail response, laced with frustration and indignation (known in some associations as a "nastygram"). Of course, you made sure to copy a few colleagues and/or supervisors, so everyone could see how correct your point was.

The problem is, the e-mail response you then get from your colleague is even nastier, and includes a now expanded list of recipients. You'll be frustrated because for some reason your colleague did not address the rational points you made in your e-mail—he brought in new points that are only distractions to the issue at hand! You'd better get started on that reply e-mail. Is there any way you can copy the entire staff and board?

This pattern is all too common, and we must stop it.

Using e-mail to communicate in conflict situations never works, and it usually makes things worse, because e-mail communication is designed for simple information exchange, not complex communication. All conflict situations are complex—if they were simple, they would be resolved by now. Conflict situations require deeper communication than e-mail allows. It requires back and forth, clarification of positions, examination of assumptions, and communication at the level of logic and emotion at the same time.

You can't do that with e-mail, because there is no tone. When two people talk to each other, most of the meaning is conveyed in nonverbal communication, particularly the use of tone. Which words you emphasize and the pattern of raising or lowering tone as you speak is absolutely critical for people to know what you really mean. Consider the following point you made in your e-mail:

"Things were going great, and then Bob came into the room."

The reader of the e-mail has to figure out what you mean. On one hand, you might have felt that things were actually going poorly (you were being sarcastic by saying they were great), and you wanted to make a point about how relieved you were that Bob came in the room to save the day. On the other hand, you might have meant that things really were going great—until the moment Bob came in, and it clearly it went downhill from there. The only way the e-mail recipient would know which of these two drastically different meanings is accurate would be through your tone (which does not exist on e-mail), or by context. That is, if they already know that you don't like Bob, they will guess that you were implying that things were going downhill.

So not only do e-mails rob communication of tone, making the communication inherently more confusing, they also force the recipient to determine what you mean *based on their previous knowledge of who you are and what you think.* In conflict situations, that is not likely to be an accurate (or pretty) picture, so they are even more likely to interpret what you are saying in the worst possible way. Clicking the "send" button on an e-mail in a conflict situation is like clicking on an automatic "escalate" button.

The answer, of course, is to not send the e-mail. Walk down the hall. Pick up the phone. Make it the norm in your association to de-escalate the conflict when you get that frustrating e-mail by responding directly, instead of through a nasty-gram. It may take a bit more time in the short term (and you will need to brush up on your conflict resolution and communication skills), but it will save volumes of time in the long run by enabling quicker and more direct resolution of conflict.

CHANGING THE WAY WE INVOLVE OTHERS

Sometimes Research Is Not Enough

Mickie Rops

So the story goes: Sony held a focus group to determine if they should make their new boom box yellow or black. They invited in their target demographic (teenagers) to ask their opinion. The focus group was unanimously in favor of yellow—as it was "hip," "edgy" and "cool." As a thank you gift for participating, all were offered a new boom box. There was a table covered with yellow and black boom boxes. Everyone took a black one. So, Sony made their new boom box black.

While I don't know if this is urban legend or truth, it has stuck with me for years and illustrates a good point: Customers don't always know and/or articulate what they really want or need. Yet, how often do associations base decisions solely or primarily on survey or focus group results? We ask members to choose topics for the next conference from a long list of possible topics, we ask if they would value some vague concept of a program we are considering, we ask if they would buy a certain product a year from now, and we ask what would increase the value of membership. But sometimes our questions are loaded and members tell us what they think we want to hear or they just don't tell us anything at all. Sometimes our questions are just too vague for meaningful responses. Sometimes members just don't know what they want. Sometimes they don't know how to communicate their needs to us.

It is important to recognize the inherent flaws in the research methodologies we often use to gather the data on which we base decisions. We need to figure out ways to gather more authentic data from members—through better questions in our research, but also through:

- observations of their actions.
- listening to their conversations.
- engaging in meaningful conversations with them.

May I Have Your Attention Please!

David Gammel

How much attention do your members pay to you? Many web-oriented companies and services have begun thinking about how much of their customers' attention they receive rather than how much of their money they get. This is described as attention economics.

Framing your products and services within the concept of gaining attention may help you to better target your members' interests and ultimately increase revenue and member satisfaction over the long run.

Some attention questions to ask about your association:

- How much of our members' attention do we want?
- How much should we have?
- How much do they give us now?
- What are they paying attention to?
- What will it take for our association to be front-of-mind with our members?

If you focus on getting and retaining your members' attention, the money will follow.

Custom Memberships

Amy Smith

What would happen if there were a dedicated person within your membership department whose entire focus was to create custom membership packages for your members and prospects?

Custom memberships? No way? Read on.

Let's take a look at package membership categories and what these offer your prospective members. ASAE & The Center for Association Leadership have been offering Circle Club memberships for several years now. They offer membership packages at various price points, depending on how many staff members need to participate. The package includes annual dues for a number of people plus registration for the annual conference or Great Ideas, all of the virtual seminars and other education programs offered through CenterU. It is really easy to look at the programming calendar and realize that the minimum (bronze) level membership of $2,000 is a great deal if you participate in a fair number of CenterU programs.

The eLearning Guild (www.elearningguild.com) just instituted similar types of membership categories in that access depends on what you pay. They have four membership categories ranging from free to $1,695 per year. Each gives you progressively more access to online resources and educational program.

Both of these programs are a great step in the right direction. But what if, at the time of the renewal, your membership director analyzes the member's activity for the year, crafts the foundation for a customized membership, calls the member to consult with them on their needs for the coming year, finalizes a custom package based on member feedback and renews that member for the coming year? And what if that customization provides a 20% or greater increase in dues revenue?

I would argue that more often than not three things will happen in this process: (1) your membership director will begin to see membership benefit trends, (2) members will appreciate and highly value the personal attention, and (3) members will begin to take advantage of a wider range of programs and services offered by the association.

Members Do Not Own the Association

Jeff De Cagna

Let's be clear about something really important: **The members don't *really* own the association.** The overwhelming majority of associations are structured as non-profit organizations and there can be neither individual nor group ownership of such entities. Non-profit organizations exist for the public good, and not for personal or private aggrandizement.

I think all association professionals should keep this in mind the next time they are asked to defer their day-to-day experience, marketplace insight and strategic judgment to the myopic and closed-off decision-making of volunteers who, more and more, lack the time, energy and attention to attend to association business properly. I am deeply concerned that if we continue to buy into the outmoded belief that it is "the members' association," we will be complicit in driving our organizations down the pathways of extinction.

I'm not suggesting that the members don't play the central roles in determining what occurs within the organizations to which they belong. Not at all. Without the direct, substantive and active engagement of members in the association, there is simply no possibility for long-term success. But just as important is the direct, substantive and active involvement of staff, partners and other stakeholders on a co-equal basis. Associations are not manufacturers of widgets, but creators of knowledge, experiences and context. We cannot effectively cultivate and nurture these intangible resources in command-and-control hierarchies in which some lead and others follow. Instead, this work demands highly diverse and collaborative environments in which leadership and followership are shared by all in equal measure.

No one owns the association, but everyone involved in its work takes ownership of its success or failure every day. Our community is long overdue in recognizing this fundamental fact.

Walking the Community Talk

David Gammel

Many associations profess that their focus is on fostering community among their members for the purpose of facilitating knowledge sharing and other professionally enhancing activities. ASAE even came out with a report recommending building community driven membership benefits.

Yet, many of these same associations limit or even discourage their staff from participating in similar activities. Some do not encourage staff to use time in the office to engage in online communities or skimp on professional development. Others specifically block access to unauthorized websites and limit the ability to use tools such as instant messaging. How can they reasonably expect their staff to develop effective and powerful community-based experiences for their members when they do not encourage their staff to engage in such activities themselves?

Association executives must encourage their staff and leadership to experiment with and model the behaviors and actions they want to elicit from their membership. Any association that does not do that will ultimately fail in their community efforts, because they honestly won't be able recognize it.

Taking a Measure of Member Mood

MICKIE ROPS

In the March 2006 issue of Harvard Business Review, a short article described how the nationally known restaurant at the Inn at Little Washington (www.theinnatlittlewashington.com) takes a measure of each guest table's mood on a scale of one to ten, with seven or below indicating displeasure or unhappiness. The mood score is recorded in the computer and the goal is to get that measure to at least a nine by the end of the meal. The strategies might include complimentary champagne, extra desserts, a tableside visit from one of the owners, or even a kitchen tour. A personal favorite: if a wife looks annoyed that the husband is paying a little too much attention to a well-endowed waitress, a waiter takes over.

Consider what the member experience might look like if associations similarly targeted member mood during each interaction. Have you ever had secret shoppers assess how your staff members are treating members on the phone, at busy conference registration tables, or elsewhere? You might just be shocked at how often the member mood is depressed rather than elevated during these interactions. Too often, calling members are repeatedly transferred, unable to find a real person to talk to, or told no to their simple requests. About the only measure of mood associations take of members is through customer satisfaction surveys and conference evaluations. But isn't that too little too late? Wouldn't it be more effective to enter every interaction aiming to elevate the member mood?

How often do your members leave the interaction feeling *great* about the experience? Consider how you might be able to apply the measure of mood concept to your organization.

Membership Benefits Like Software Upgrades

AMY SMITH

Software companies create releases for a wide range of reasons. But one of those is to stay ahead of the competition. What if we started to think about membership benefits much like software upgrades? For example, the strategy would be to come up with membership benefit upgrade releases each quarter.

This would require three things: (1) a listing of each of the current member benefits, (2) an ongoing assessment of how each of these benefits are utilized (quantitative) and viewed (qualitative) by members, and (3) gathering of new benefits that members would like.

Now keep in mind that each quarter some of these upgrades may be minor and others may be major.

Here's just one brainstorm on the possibilities:

Release 1.0—the list of benefits your organization currently offers now and a clear communication campaign to gather data on these benefits and new ones that members want.

Release 1.1—after a quarterly analysis, you drop a few of the non-performing benefits and add a couple of moderate benefits.

Release 1.2—you drop a few more of the least performing benefits and add a couple of great new ones.

Release 1.3—you continue to drop the least performing benefits and add a significant new benefit. (Now it's time for a member to think about renewing.)

Release 1.4—it's been a year, so you restate the benefits added to date, add another new benefit or two.

Release 2.0—create your new list of benefits for the year, communicate what's coming in the next release, drop a few, add a few…

Very quickly your organization will really be in tune with your membership. Old and unused programs and services will be dropped, and new ones will take their place. Good programs that simply need a tune up are updated and scheduled for release.

The best part is that the decisions are business related, not personal or worst of all, "because we've always done it that way."

Avoiding Clarity About Who Is in Charge

Jamie Notter

We sometimes hear leaders in associations from both the staff side and the volunteer side debating the pros and cons of being "member driven" versus "staff driven." We have yet to hear a compelling argument that rules definitively in favor of one over the other. It seems to vary by context, with the bottom line containing an unsurprising mix of responsibilities for driving divided between staff and members.

The debate over staff versus member driven, however, is really just a reframing of the more basic question: Who is in charge? And while we agree that there is no singular or simple answer to that question at the macro level (the macro answer is "it depends"), this should not provide association leaders with an excuse for avoiding this question within their own, specific, micro-level situations.

To be successful, association leaders must clarify and pinpoint a specific answer to that question within their own context. That is not just at the Board meetings, where the staff versus member paradigm would expect the topic to come up. Confusion about who is in charge appears elsewhere in the association's business as well.

Staff

Association leaders often espouse flat organizations, valuing input from everyone, even suggesting consensus decision making. At the same time, however, they structure their organizations hierarchically, where reporting relationships define authority in a clear and vertical fashion. You must confront this contradiction so staff will understand when they have input and when they do not. There is room for broad input, but do not hide the fact that a very few actually have the decision making power on major questions. You need not concentrate all control in the hands of the managers, but be truthful and clear about areas where control is not shared, and everyone will work more effectively.

Related Organizations

When associations create related organizations (often driven by benefits of a different tax status), they too often create independent Boards and structures of organizations that they intend to be literally subsidiaries of the association. It is easy to focus on the purpose of the new organization, its mission, and empowering the new Board that is set up to lead effectively, and in doing so avoid the "who's in charge" question entirely. The two Boards then operate for years, even decades, without confronting huge contradictions in expectations and purpose. Each Board feels it is in charge, yet it never confronts the issue head on.

It takes courage to confront these "who is in charge" conversations. But remember, while the conversations may be difficult, they won't kill you, and the longer you put off having them, the more difficult they will be.

Social Media Are Like Manna from Heaven

Jeff De Cagna

There is now a genuine interest in associations around blogging, podcasting and social media tools. **FINALLY!** We are long overdue to recognize these technologies are like manna from heaven for associations, and to begin applying them strategically to our work.

Social media are all about participation, about getting people involved in creating and sharing content and engaging in conversations that are important to them. Indeed, the whole direction of the Web is moving toward the deeper engagement of the end user in more authentic and generative ways. In this spirit, blogging, podcasting, wikis, as well as sites such as Flickr (photo sharing) and del.icio.us (social bookmarking/tagging), offer associations the opportunity to establish entirely new relationships with their current and prospective members. By introducing greater richness and texture to the discourse we have with our most crucial stakeholders, we can quite possibly renovate for the better the eroding value propositions of traditional association membership offers and volunteer leadership participation.

But this will happen only if we can get out of our own way. Going forward, associations will need to do more than pay lip service to the passion, energy and creativity of their members and staff. Going forward, associations will need to reconsider the long-term importance of the current incentives that motivate members to invest their discretionary time and attention in the organization. Associations, by definition, are highly bureaucratic organizations. And, in the words of strategy and innovation author Gary Hamel, "the problem is, there's little room in bureaucratic organizations for passion, ingenuity and self-direction." Social media are the antithesis of bureaucracy. Social media are pure creation.

We have been given a gift, like manna from heaven. Let us not squander it.

Going Social with Your Public Service Announcements

David Gammel

Many associations create public service announcement videos (PSAs) highlighting important issues on behalf of their members to the general public. However, PSAs are often run by television stations during low ratings time slots to use up excess advertising capacity that they were not able to sell. Hardly ideal exposure.

Enter YouTube, the online video sharing service that was founded in 2005. Anyone can post video to the site, which then allows others to comment and rate the video as well as share it via e-mail and blogs with their friends. Corporate marketers have recently begun posting video clips to the site as part of their marketing. They also peruse the comments people add to the videos as a research tool for how people react to the videos.

Associations should experiment with using services such as YouTube to get their ideas out into the greater web community. Be prepared to view the feedback you get on your video as valuable insight into how people react to your piece without getting defensive. Ultimately, sharing video via services such as YouTube may get your PSA much more exposure to higher quality audiences than traditional distribution can provide.

The real innovation will come, however, when your members begin posting their own video testimonials and commentary about your field on their own initiative!

RSS and Learning

AMY SMITH

If you are responsible for learning, education, professional development, training, communications or PR and have not explored the world of RSS, you really need to.

Check out www.feeddemon.com or any of the other common RSS services (Google RSS Feeds to find a listing). You'll quickly see how powerful this tool is. The beauty of it is that it is a user defined tool, meaning the user determines what sites (and specific sections/pages) are fed into the reader.

It is a great way to stay on top of blogs and websites of interest to you. You categorize them in a way that makes sense to you. For example, one of my categories is "Association Blogs." There I have a listing of about sixteen or so blogs from a wide range of authors. I have another category called "eLearning Blogs" where I have about twenty-five blogs and websites that I track (that have RSS feeds). What's great is that there is a "newspaper" feature that pulls the headlines from the entire category of blogs (all twenty-five for example) onto one page, so I can quickly scan through titles and see what's being talked about.

Why can't you help facilitate something similar for your members?

How about creating a web page that simply lists the RSS feeds from your industry/profession? Your organization now becomes the knowledge center for your industry or profession, and you don't have to offer all of the content.

"Knowledgizing" Associations

Mickie Rops

Why haven't more associations figured out that the impact of pushing content out to members is limited? Google any key word in your industry and the search will likely yield thousands (if not millions) of hits. The fingertip knowledge of our members is immense, yet associations keep utilizing precious resources to crank even more of it out—newsletters full of articles on anything authors volunteer to write, conference CDs (or audiotapes, if you can believe it) for every conference session, and conference sessions selected from whatever came in through the call for proposals.

Associations need to move beyond being pushers of information, and strive to be facilitators of knowledge creation and sharing.

How do we do that? Here are four strategies for "knowledgizing" associations—filtering, feedback, context and connections.

Filtering is extracting from the information masses only the relevant information for a particular audience. A few examples:

- Prioritizing key content areas (in which members face challenges, where contradictory or vast research exists, etc.) and engaging experts in the field to filter out the nuggets and/or summarize findings and trends
- Providing opt-in headliner e-mails that contain current news headlines about the industry that are linked to the actual articles (for broad fields, these can be issue-specific)
- Website personalization (providing additional relevant content to members based on identified preferences or actions—think Amazon.com)
- Selling customized versions of your industry research (by industry segment, for example, rather than the full data set)

Bottom line value: Save your members time by filtering out the excess or irrelevant.

Providing **feedback** means offering a constructive and informative response to the results of an activity. Examples include:

- Coaching or mentoring programs
- Self-assessments with guided learning (that provide the correct answer and a detailed rationale)
- Learning quizzes with guided learning within publications and courses
- Template checklists and evaluation forms for members to use with their supervisors or peers to gather feedback on their performance

Bottom line value: Members don't always know what they don't know; help them to discover it.

Providing context is adding meaning to content by relating it to specific circumstances. Examples include:

- An online interactive practice journal where specific cases are described and questions are presented within a chat or discussion forum
- Plan coordinated curriculum learning events (as stand-alones and as conference tracks)
- Provide pre-conference recommended readings to attendees to set the stage for the material they are about to learn
- Encourage speakers/e-learning faculty to build meaningful case studies and problem-solving activities into their sessions/courses
- Build opportunities for both structured and unstructured peer-to-peer sharing into events

Bottom line value: Help members turn content into knowledge.

Facilitating **connections** is bringing together individuals with common interests, issues or expertise. Examples include:

- Coaching or mentoring programs
- Communities of practice
- Online group collaboration (wikis, chats, discussion lists)
- Social networking systems
- Incorporating connection time and activities in association events

Bottom line value: Connections enable shared context and build community, both key to establishing a knowledge sharing environment.

When A Member Wants to Give You Money, Get Out of the Way

DAVID GAMMEL

Many associations collect demographic data from their members when they join or renew their membership. Sometimes this can be as simple as a few check boxes to more involved multi-page surveys. When dues invoices could only be sent via postal mail, it made sense to piggy back a data collection tool with it to save money on postage and take advantage of the member's attention.

However, just because it works well in snail mail doesn't mean you should do it online. For example, the cost-saving benefit goes away when you invoice for dues via e-mail or accept a new member via your website. Another challenge is that conducting an online survey of a member before they can renew is much more invasive of an interruption than including a paper form in the mail. Making online payment challenging by requiring extraneous forms to be completed reduces the benefits of paying online to your members, which will raise your costs when they choose to go with traditional methods such as calling you or mailing in forms that need to be processed.

When a member has made the decision to invest more money in the association by purchasing a product or paying dues online, get out of their way and make it as easy as possible for them to complete the transaction.

Your Members Are Subject Matter Experts

AMY SMITH

All of your members are subject matter experts. So why are we still offering conference sessions where there is a sage on the stage? And how is it that reprinting PowerPoint slides two, three or six to a page is considered okay as a handout? How much great information is lost during a session because there is no way to collect useful tips, tricks and resources that are in the heads of participants, let alone the speaker?

Enter, the wiki!

Learning guru Elliott Masie's Learning2006 conference has done a great job pushing the subject matter responsibilities out to the conference participants. He also has big names participating (and helping to draw in attendees).

The site is www.learning2006.com. We are so big on this conference because:

(1) It is a for-profit entity successfully competing (and we would argue winning) the audience in the education technology conference space.
(2) It is highly experimental, and thus, successful.
(3) It provides huge value to attendees.

What's more, they already have 714 people registered, and there are only a handful of thought leaders announced on the conference's home page. They haven't even announced the session topics!

Last year we had about ten association executives at the conference. Besides learning a lot about education technology from colleagues outside of the association space, the conference is a great case study in, well, conferencing, especially from a marketing perspective.

No More Committees

Jeff De Cagna

While attending a conference on innovation, I began thinking about things we can do to increase the likelihood of innovation in our organizations. Of course, there are many steps we can take, but it occurred to me that **eliminating all standing committees** is a simple, high impact idea.

Individually, each association committee is a pocket of bureaucracy. The totality of an association's committee structure is the underpinning of an organization's "infrastructure of the status quo." So let's shake it up! Here is a prescription for an alternative architecture of "collaborative groups" that I think can work for virtually every association:

1. No more than six to eight members per group
2. An equal number of staff and volunteers working together
3. No chairs; co-facilitators, one staff and one volunteer rotating on a monthly basis
4. A duration of no less than three months and no more than four months
5. The ability to reorganize and continue working at the end (but it must turnover at least half of its membership)
6. No reports, only conversations
7. Mutual evaluations; everyone in a group gets to evaluate the contributions of every other member.

The idea here is to change the dynamics of collaboration and decision-making in associations by challenging the assumptions of how staff and volunteers should relate. True creativity and innovation emerges when there is shared respect for a diversity of views and "who's in charge" is much less important than "who's got a great idea?"

If we're going to work on projects, we should work on them and complete them as quickly and intelligently as possible. If the original group

---

assigned to work on something can't get it done, then new people should be incorporated because new ideas likely are required. The result of group work shouldn't be a report, but some set of outcomes. The role of the group should be engaging others in conversations about them to ensure they are the right outcomes.

Finally, this more flexible architecture should make it possible to develop both staff and volunteers as leaders, and move them around to a variety of learning opportunities. The only way that we will help our people grow is by giving them feedback on where they already excel and where they need to do further work. Who better than group colleagues to do such evaluation?

Now, before you come up with a hundred different objections to the idea, let me invite you instead to try and improve it. Ask yourself this question: **How could this work?** That's the way to take innovation in a positive direction in your organization.

It's All About the Value

Mickie Rops

How often do association executives or volunteer leaders say that they can't raise the member dues because their members can't afford it or won't pay it? How many times each year do those same members spend an amount equal or greater than that dues payment for something else? A conference registration? A certification? A suit? A purse? A set of golf clubs or a round of golf? Tickets to a theatre series? A weekend getaway? You get the idea.

I once sat through a dreadful house of delegates' meeting of an association that was, at the time, in a dire financial situation. Delegate after delegate pronounced that the association just could not raise dues because the members could not afford it and would drop membership. They spent the full meeting discussing why the membership couldn't afford it, what billing options could be instituted, what programs could be cut instead, etc. Not once did I hear the suggestion that perhaps the organization could consider ways to increase its value for the dollar. Not once.

More often than not, it is not about the actual dollar amount. It is about the perceived value of what members are getting for it. **If there's little to no real value in membership, then any fee is too high.**

Free Shipping for Members Instead of Discounted Prices

David Gammel

Amazon.com sells a membership called Amazon Prime. Membership gets you free two-day shipping and discounts on sending packages overnight. The more you spend with Amazon, the more valuable your membership. It is very easy to understand the value of the membership because it is quite simple. You can even share the member benefits with up to four other people in your household. Nice dynamic!

Why not offer free shipping to your members for all publications and products rather than giving a discount off the price? Discounting your products can be seen as devaluing their worth. Free shipping is an excellent perk that doesn't make any statement about the worth of the content and encourages more spending. It should also make you more money in the long run since it is roughly a fixed cost and you won't be discounting your more expensive items.

Conclusion: 102 and Counting

Most association publications finish with an inspirational and somewhat serious conclusion. Having delivered our many pages of provocation, we should now lower our voices just a little, slow our cadence just a touch, and deliver that powerful statement that will leave you with that "Wow, that was a great presentation!" feeling.

There is only one problem: **that is how we have always done it.**

The "basking in our own wisdom" conclusion is a classic in this field, but it does nothing to inspire change. It may make us feel better, but the only action it is likely to generate is placing this book back on the shelf. If you have read this book through to the end, you should realize by now that we will do the conclusion differently.

This is not the end; this is the beginning. You know as well as we do that there are far, far more than 101 things in the association community we must change, and our greatest hope is that you have already tried to identify numbers 102 and beyond. Please take what we have written, and run with it. Develop new experiments. Start new conversations with Board members, staff or other stakeholders. Transform our provocative ideas into your own challenges to the status quo.

Please let us know how it works out by visiting our blog at http://www.alwaysdoneitthatway.com. Please share with us what you are learning, and we promise to honor your work by taking it up another notch. Working together we are confident that we can accelerate the emergence of a fundamentally new approach to association leadership.

So what is your next step?

The Anti-Status-Quo Leader's Reading List

WARNING: THESE BOOKS MAY BE HAZARDOUS TO "ALWAYS DONE IT THAT WAY" THINKING. PROCEED AT YOUR OWN RISK!

Anderson, Chris, *The Long Tail: Why the Future of Business is Selling Less of More* (Hyperion, 2006).

Battelle, John, *The Search: How Google and Its Rivals Rewrote the Rules of Business and Transformed Our Culture* (Portfolio, 2005).

Block, Peter, *The Answer to How is Yes: Acting on What Matters* (Berrett-Koehler Publishers, Inc., 2002).

Buckingham, Marcus and Donald O. Clifton, *Now, Discover Your Strengths* (The Free Press, 2001).

Carr, Nicholas G., *Does IT Matter? Information Technology and the Corrosion of Competitive Advantage* (Harvard Business School Press, 2004).

Chesbrough, Henry, *Open Innovation: The New Imperative for Creating and Profiting from Technology* (Harvard Business School Press, 2003).

Collins, Jim, *Good to Great: Why Some Companies Make the Leap and Others Don't* (HarperCollins, 2002).

Cross, Rob and Andrew Parker, *The Hidden Power of Social Networks: Understanding How Work Really Gets Done in Organizations* (Harvard Business School Press, 2004).

Friedman, Thomas, *The World Is Flat: A Brief History of the Twenty-first Century* (Farrar, Straus and Giroux, 2005).

Gladwell, Malcolm, *The Tipping Point: How Little Things Can Make a Big Difference* (Little Brown & Co., 2000).

Goleman, Daniel, Annie McKee and Richard Boyatzis, *Primal Leadership: Realizing the Power of Emotional Intelligence* (Harvard Business School Press, 2002).

Hagel, John and John Seely Brown, *The Only Sustainable Edge: Why Business Strategy Depends on Productive Friction and Dynamic Specialization* (Harvard Business School Press, 2005).

Hamel, Gary, *Leading the Revolution: How to Thrive in Turbulent Times by Making Innovation a Way of Life* (Harvard Business School Press, 2002).

Hargadon, Andrew, *How Breakthroughs Happen: The Surprising Truth About How Companies Innovate* (Harvard Business School Press, 2003).

Heifetz, Ronald A, *Leadership Without Easy Answers* (Harvard University Press, 1994).

Johansson, Frans, *The Medici Effect: Breakthrough Insights at the Intersection of Ideas, Concepts & Cultures* (Harvard Business School Press, 2004).

Katzenbach, Jon and Douglas Smith, *The Wisdom of Teams: Creating the High-Performance Organization* (HarperCollins, 1999).

Kelley, Tom with Jonathan Littman, *The Art of Innovation: Lessons in Creativity from IDEO, America's Leading Design Firm* (Currency, 2001).

Kelley, Tom with Jonathan Littman, *The Ten Faces of Innovation: IDEO's Strategies for Defeating the Devil's Advocate and Driving Creativity Throughout Your Organization* (Currency, 2005).

Kim, W. Chan and Renee Mauborgne, *Blue Ocean Strategy: How to Create Uncontested Market Space and Make the Competition Irrelevant* (Harvard Business School Press, 2005).

Kleiner, Art, *Who Really Matters: The Core Group Theory of Power, Privilege, and Success* (Doubleday, 2003).

Kouzes, James M. and Barry Z. Posner, *The Leadership Challenge: How to Keep Getting Extraordinary Things Done in Organizations* (Jossey-Bass, 1995).

Lencioni, Patrick, *The Five Dysfunctions of a Team: A Leadership Fable* (Jossey-Bass, 2002).

Lencioni, Patrick, *Death by Meeting: A Leadership Fable About Solving the Most Painful Problem in Business* (Jossey-Bass, 2004).

Levitt, Steven D. and Stephen J. Dubner, *Freakonomics : A Rogue Economist Explores the Hidden Side of Everything* (William Morrow, 2005).

MacKenzie, Gordon, *Orbiting the Giant Hairball: A Corporate Fool's Guide to Surviving with Grace* (Viking, 1996).

Malone, Thomas W., *The Future of Work: How the New Order of Business Will Shape Your Organization, Your Management Style and Your Life* (Harvard Business School Press, 2004).

Peters, Tom, *Re-imagine!* (DK ADULT, 2003).

Peters, Tom, *The Circle of Innovation: You Can't Shrink Your Way to Greatness* (Knopf, 1997).

Pfeffer, Jeffrey and Robert I. Sutton, *The Knowing-Doing Gap: How Smart Companies Turn Knowledge into Action* (Harvard Business School Press, 2000).

Pink, Daniel H., *A Whole New Mind: Moving from the Information Age to the Conceptual Age* (Riverhead, 2005).

Senge, Peter, *The Fifth Discipline: The Art and Practice of the Learning Organization* (Currency Doubleday, 1990).

Schein, Edgar. *The Corporate Culture Survival Guide: Sense and Nonsense About Culture Change* (Jossey-Bass, 1999).

Scoble, Robert and Shel Israel, *Naked Conversations: How Blogs are Changing the Way Businesses Talk with Customers* (Wiley, 2006).

Stone, Douglas, Bruce Patton, and Sheila Heen, *Difficult Conversations: How to Discuss What Matters Most* (Penguin Books, 1999).

Vise, David and Mark Malseed, *The Google Story* (Delacore Press, 2005).

von Hippel, Eric, *Democratizing Innovation* (The MIT Press, 2005).

Wenger, Etienne, Richard McDermott, and William M. Snyder, *Cultivating Communities of Practice: A Guide to Managing Knowledge* (Harvard Business School Press, 2002).

Wheatley, Margaret, *Finding Our Way: Leadership for an Uncertain Time* (Berrett-Koehler Publishers, Inc., 2005).

Contents, By Author

Jamie Notter

Amy Smith

About the Authors

JEFF DE CAGNA
jeff@principledinnovation.com
jeff@associationrenewal.com

Jeff De Cagna—*the association community's leading voice for innovation*—is chief strategist and founder of Principled Innovation LLC, located in Reston, Virginia. Widely recognized as one of the association community's preeminent thought leaders, Jeff is a Fellow of ASAE & The Center for Association Leadership, and is serving as the Chair of ASAE & The Center's Executive Management Section Council during the 2006–2007 year. He has also served on the Professional Development Section Council and the *Journal of Association Leadership* Editorial Advisory Board, and was the publication's founding managing editor. He blogs and podcasts on the Principled Innovation Blog at http://www.principledinnovationblog.com. Jeff is a graduate of The Johns Hopkins University and earned a master's degree at Harvard University.

C. DAVID GAMMEL
david@highcontext.com

David Gammel, CAE, was one of the first association executives to begin blogging about his work with the Web, knowledge management and membership organizations. David is a recognized leader in the association field on topics related to the Web and is a past Chairman of the ASAE Technology Section Council. David's consulting firm, High

Context Consulting LLC, assists both associations and corporations with focusing their Web and knowledge efforts on contributing significantly to their overall goals as an organization.

JAMIE NOTTER

jamie@notterconsulting.com
jamie@associationrenewal.com

Jamie Notter has been writing, speaking, and consulting in the association community since 2001. Jamie runs his own consulting practice, Notter Consulting, which helps leaders to master the human side of their organizations. In 2005 he teamed up with fellow author Jeff De Cagna to start Association Renewal LLC, a consulting company that delivers next generation leadership to associations, today. Jamie began his career in the international conflict resolution field and has completed graduate programs in conflict resolution and organization development.

MICKIE ROPS

mickie@msrops.com

Mickie S. Rops, CAE—a highly regarded advisor on knowledge and credentialing strategy—helps associations create programs of sustainable value through staff/leadership training, coaching, strategy development, research/white papers, and program audits. Mickie is the author of over 25 association industry publications, including ASAE & The Center's only book devoted to association knowledge, *Identifying and Using a Field's Body of Knowledge*, the certification chapter in *Core Competencies in Professional Development*, and *The Certification Toolkit*. Her blog, the first and only one devoted to association knowledge and credentialing, can be read at http://msrops.blogs.com/.

Amy Smith
amysmith@amysmithconsulting.com

As a former association educator, Amy Smith brings association education experience, adult learning expertise, and an education technology Master's degree to her client projects. As President & Chief Learning Officer of Amy Smith Consulting, LLC, her vendor-neutral firm designs high-impact learning strategies for associations and non-profits. Amy works with a wide range of organizations to design effective learning experiences to maximize the benefits of technology while valuing the face-to-face experience. A leader in association eLearning, Amy is a frequent speaker and authored the education technology chapter in the ASAE book, *Core Competencies in Professional Development.*